PROTECT
YOUR
401(k)

PROTECT YOUR 401(k)

10 Steps You Must Take to Protect
Your Retirement Nest Egg

Larry Chambers
Ken Ziesenheim

McGraw-Hill

New York Chicago San Francisco Lisbon Madrid
Mexico City Milan New Delhi San Juan
Seoul Singapore Sydney Toronto

Library of Congress Cataloging-in-Publication Data

Chambers, Larry.
  Protect your 401(k): 10 steps you must take to protect your retirement nest
egg / by Larry Chambers and Ken Ziesenheim.
    p. cm.
  ISBN 0-07-140712-X (pbk.: alk. paper)
    1. 401(k) plans—management. 2. Portfolio management—United States. 3.
Retirement income—United States—planning. I. Ziesenheim, Ken. II. Title.
  HD7105.45.U^ C435 2002
  332.024'01—dc21
                            2002005271

McGraw-Hill

A Division of The **McGraw·Hill** Companies

1 2 3 4 5 6 7 8 9 0 DOC/DOC 0 9 8 7 6 5 4 3 2

ISBN 0-07-140712-X

*The sponsoring editor is Stephen Isaacs. Production services provided by CWL
Publishing Enterprises, Inc., Madison, Wisconsin, www.cwlpub.com.*

Printed and bound by R. R. Donnelley & Sons Company.

This publication is designed to provide accurate and authoritative information in
regard to the subject matter covered. It is sold with the understanding that neither the author nor the publisher is engaged in rendering legal, accounting, or
other professional service. If legal advice or other expert assistance is required,
the services of a competent professional person should be sought.
                —*From a Declaration of Principles jointly*
                  adopted by a Committee of the American Bar
                  Association and a Committee of Publishers

McGraw-Hill books are available at special quantity discounts to use as premi-
ums and sales promotions, or for use in corporate training programs. For more
information, please write to the Director of Special Sales, McGraw-Hill, 2
Penn Plaza, New York, NY 10121. Or contact your local bookstore.

 This book is printed on recycled, acid-free paper containing a minimum of 50% recycled de-inked fiber.

Contents

Preface

WE HAVE ENTERED THE "Era of Personal Responsibility"—and many of us have done so unprepared and unknowledgeable. Except for the unusual bull market of the '90s, which drew millions of new people into the world of investing, we have paid little attention to the need to accumulate wealth for our future needs. Gone are the days of pension plans controlled by your employer with inflation-adjusted benefits. Here to stay are longer life spans, higher housing and medical costs, and a disintegration of the family unit as a support structure for the elderly. Your retirement investing is now up to you!

For the beginner, this may be a difficult challenge, but it's not really all that hard. Of course, it requires that you put in some time understanding your investments. The purpose of this book is to show you how and give you hope. By applying some tried-and-true techniques, your money will be there when you need it—perhaps to the tune of more than a million dollars!

In this book, you'll learn how to make this happen by taking full advantage of the opportunities presented by your participation in a 401(k) plan. You'll see why it's not such a good idea to have a lot of your money, for example, in the stock of the company you work for, as the employees of Enron, Global Crossing, Lucent Technology, and World.com unhappily discovered too late. We will help you see the value of "paying yourself" before you pay others and why you need to max out your contributions (if you can) to your 401(k) plan and therefore max out the matching contributions from your employer into the plan.

And once you've started making contributions, we'll help you understand how to make the best decisions for where to invest your money, given your tolerance for risk, your time horizon, and your financial goals. You'll learn about the risks (and returns) associated with different types of investments, from government bonds to small-cap international funds. You'll find a clear, basic description of what we call "the six concepts of successful investing," including diversification, asset class investing, and portfolio rebalancing. If you're a beginner, we know this sounds like "stockbroker speak," but it's not really all that complicated, and the disciplined application of these concepts can mean big payoffs for you when you're ready to retire.

After you get the basics of investing, we provide you with the information you'll need to make the best decisions about the funds you want your money invested in to meet your financial goals. Do you want a conservative, balanced, growth, or aggressive portfolio? Each has its advantages, and we'll give you the background you need to make informed and intelligent decisions.

If you need advice or help in managing your investments, we provide a chapter on where you can find it and choose the kind of help that will be best for you. Finally, when it's time to cash in and retire (or you need the money for some other purpose), we explain how to do that safely and in a way that will make the money last.

ESOP, ERISA, qualified plans—there are a lot of terms dealing with the investments and legalities associated with 401(k) plans. Therefore, at the end of the book, you'll find a comprehensive glossary that explains these terms in a straightforward and useful manner.

This book is relatively short as investment books go, but that is intentional. It covers the basics, provides a variety of useful examples, but never gets too technical. By applying the basic principles described here, you can be one of the winners in the 401(k) sweepstakes. And we're glad to be able to help you make that happen.

Acknowledgments

Various people and organizations have assisted us in the preparation of this book. We'd like to thank *Mutual Funds* magazine and Lynn O'Shaughnessy for several charts and data that appear here. Joe Duran, CFA, and co-author of *The First Time Investor's Workbook*, also generously provided us with his insights as well as several figures. For his contribution of the "Pay Yourself First" chapter, we wish to thank James E. McWhinney at Lockwood Advisors, Inc. Others who have helped us and whom we would like to thank include Chip Roame of Tiburon Strategic Advisors; Len Reinhart, CEO of Lockwood Family of Companies; Bob Goodman, Senior Economist for Putnam; Susan Latremoille, The Latremoille Group, Toronto, Ontario; Mark Matson in Cincinnati, Ohio; and Carl Krietsch at Lockwood Advisors, Inc. And special thanks to Karen Johnson who read and edited the manuscript as we were preparing it.

We want to express our appreciation to the Profit Sharing /401(k) Council of America for allowing us to reprint their glossary as Appendix C to this book.

We also want to thank Robert Magnan of CWL Publishing Enterprises for his help in editing the final manuscript that has become this book.

AMERICANS' NEW MOST VALUABLE ASSET!

TECHNICALLY, A 401(K) PLAN IS A DEFINED contribution retirement plan sponsored by firms for their employees. These plans allow workers to save for retirement in accounts invested in corporate equities (stocks) and bonds, as well as cash. Contributions, interest, dividends, and growth may compound tax-free until distribution in retirement.

In recent years, 401(k) accounts have grown with such speed and popularity that they are displacing traditional defined benefit pension plans.[1] The root of the 401(k)'s success is that each investor owns and controls his or her individual account. Payroll deduction, tax deferral, and employer matches have created incentives for the average American to build a liquid source of capital for the first time in the nation's history.

For many employed Americans, their 401(k) plan is now their most valuable asset, second only to their home. Sean Hanna, the publisher of 401kWire.com, explains, "It is certainly many individuals' most liquid asset. The investments can be rolled over, cashed out, borrowed against and passed down to the next generation. All these uses can be made directly, without an employer or government representative cosigning the check. Unlike capital held in the Social Security system and defined benefit system, the capital in 401(k) plans is at the beck and call of the individual worker, either individually or collectively."

> The 401(k) plan is no longer seen as just a retirement plan. They are now capital accumulation plans that fund home down payments, college tuitions, business ventures, or even a new car.

The 401(k) plan is no longer seen as just a retirement plan. They are now capital accumulation plans that fund home down payments, college tuitions, business ventures, or even a new car. Hanna tells a story about hailing a yellow cab in New York City to LaGuardia airport. A friendly chat with the driver revealed that he had purchased one of the most valuable pieces of property in Manhattan—his cab license— by tapping his 401(k). Who can argue with that?

What About All the Recent Bad Publicity?

Indeed, the Enron debacle and the poorly performing stock market over the last two years have removed some of the luster from 401(k) retirement savings plans. As equity prices surged during the past 10-year bull market run, timid investors who watched from the sidelines would suddenly decide to participate. Now they are running for safety.

Mr. 401(k) Plan Sponsor,

I just got my 401(k) account statement and I can't believe my account is down again this quarter. It has fallen from $500,000 to $400,000! I want you to do something. In the last two years, I've lost $100,000 and I can't afford to lose any more. Maybe a lot of other investments are down even more than mine are, but this is my retirement. And, don't tell me this is only normal market volatility. I can't sleep at night because I am constantly worried. Just send me my money! I'll pay the penalty!

When many 401(k) plan investors see their accounts crashing after a significant decline in value, their first thought is to abandon their investment plan, if they have any plan at all. And, switching investments because their earnings are down can do irreparable financial harm and possibly even prevent investors from ever achieving their financial goals.

The Enron scandal brought into sharp focus the vulnerability of employees' retirement accounts, especially 401(k) accounts invested in corporate stock. People are finally becoming aware that they must take steps to safeguard the assets in their 401(k) accounts, since those assets are not protected by any private or public insurance program. It is the

> **People are finally becoming aware that they must take steps to safeguard the assets in their 401(k) accounts.**

responsibility of investors to manage how their money is invested for their personal goals.

So, Why Even Bother With a 401(k)?

Why is it so important for you participate in your 401(k) and learn how to manage the assets inside this plan? Because the government is encouraging it through favorable tax legislation and your employer is motivated to support it as an employee incentive.

Plus, from an economic standpoint, the environment over the next five years for investors really couldn't be better.[2] And that prediction should come as very welcome news, because you may need more money in retirement than you planned for—a lot more. According to a study from Georgia State University,[3] household spending barely decreases when you hit the golden years. That's a jolt for 401(k) retirees who thought they'd need only 70% to 75% of their pre-retirement income. Instead, the study found that households with $40,000 in annual income saw expenses drop only $484 per year in retirement; and, those with $90,000, only $1,022. The study also found that as retiree income increased, the percentage of savings decreased. Why? Because more income increases the odds of tripping the tax on Social Security benefits for some. You may be looking at a goal of 75% to 85% (or more) of pre-retirement income as the harsh reality.

You have been given an advantage and you'd better find a way to make the most of it. You cannot let this opportunity slide past you, particularly if you are a baby boomer and therefore, part of the largest demographic group ever in the history of this country. It may be your only chance for financial independence and freedom of choice!

Learn 10 Steps to Take Immediately

Protect Your 401(k) is a practical, quick guide to the 10 steps 401(k) participants must take immediately to manage their investments and any gains they have made so far:

1. Pay Yourself First
2. Increase Your Contributions
3. Take Full Advantage of Matching Contributions
4. Know How Your Plan Works
5. Become an Informed Investor
6. Use the Six Concepts of Successful Investing
7. Understand Your Investment Vehicle Choices
8. Build a Core Investment Portfolio
9. Know Where to Get Help
10. Know How to Get Your Money Out Safely

Step 1. Pay Yourself First
When asked why participants aren't contributing to their company 401(k) plans, the most common answer is "Because I can't afford to." Unfortunately, for some people saving seems impossible: 10% is considerably more than they can afford, so they get discouraged and don't save anything. This chapter will show you where to find the money and how to start saving it.

Step 2. Increase Your Contributions

This might seem obvious, but you can't appreciate how important your contributions are until you see the consequences of not fully funding your 401(k). This chapter will demonstrate how the power and magic of compounding works with dollar cost averaging. A few extra dollars going into your 401(k) now means a whole lot extra coming out.

Automatic dollar cost averaging takes the fluctuations out of the market. When you save in a 401(k), the same amount of money comes out of your paycheck each month. So, some months this money will be invested when the markets are down, and some months you'll invest when the markets are up. Over time you should end up owning more shares at a lower price than if you had invested all your money at once. And, because your retirement account is growing through tax-deferred compounding, the more you put away, the faster it will grow. Remember the tortoise and the hare.

Step 3. Take Full Advantage of Matching Contributions

Don't turn down free money! That's what you're doing if your company offers a matching employer contribution on a 401(k) or similar retirement savings plan, but you're not participating. If you're eligible, sign up right away—don't delay! If you're not eligible, learn about the plan and your investment options and determine how much you should be saving to reach your retirement goal. Remember, an employee match is like getting a 100% return on your money!

> Don't turn down free money! That's what you're doing if your company offers a matching employer contribution on a 401(k) or similar retirement savings plan.

Step 4. Know How Your Plan Works

It's important that you learn every angle of your plan and how to work it in your favor. What are the eligibility requirements and vesting schedule? What is a "key employee"? How do the distribution rules work? Are there loan provisions? Since only you know exactly how each of these plan elements affect you, the more knowledge you have, the better chance of success you have.

Step 5. Become an Informed Investor
Don't trade in and out of the market and get saddled with fees that chip away at your returns. Don't simply default to investing for the short-term because you don't understand. Plus, you'll potentially miss out on gains that long-term investors enjoy with much less effort. Learn how to create your own personal investment plan for accumulating capital that can help you avoid investor panic and increase the possibility of achieving your financial goals.

Step 6. Use the Six Concepts of Successful Investing
There are six basic investment concepts that will give you the highest possible probability for success. This book explains how each of these concepts works together in building a plan that works in both good and bad markets. Learn these and you will reap rewards that you never dreamed possible.

- Effective Diversification
- Asset Allocation
- Asset Class Investing
- Rebalancing
- Compounding
- Long-term Investing

Step 7. Understand Your Investment Vehicle Choices
Do your homework and learn about your 401(k) investment choices. You at least need to understand why and how things work. Don't invest in anything that you don't understand and establish reasonable expectations. The problem with the bull market is that it makes people think investing is easy and guaranteed; but, truly successful investors know and understand their investment options.

Step 8. Build a Core Investment Strategy
A core strategy is the base or beginning structure of an investment portfolio that includes two or more asset classes other than cash. This term can apply to any kind of portfolio that uses fixed income (bonds) as well as equity securities to reach stated investor goals. Most mutual funds use a core strategy in selecting their initial stocks within their portfolios, as outlined in the investment objectives. Core is the base, which all investment management strategies are built on. We'll show you how to do it on your own.

Step 9. Know Where to Get Help
In my opinion, all the elements are there for another bull run for the next five years. But, you can lose money even in a bull market if you're not positioned correctly—so professional advice becomes even more important in this environment. And, since employees are completely responsible for their investment in a 401(k) plan, they have to seek professional advice.

> You can lose money even in a bull market if you're not positioned correctly—so professional advice becomes even more important in this environment.

It's important to select an advisor who has experience and knowledge, and with whom you feel compatible, just as you would your lawyer or doctor. They are just as important to your financial health.

Step 10. Know How to Get Your Money Out Safely
Learn how, by pushing your retirement age out 10 years, you can triple your 401(k) value. Don't underestimate how long you'll need your 401(k) money to last. You want it to last longer than you do, especially if you're coupled.

Because of the tax implications and inflation, *how and when* you take your money out could be more important than how you put it in. Learn the distribution rules, including any loan provisions. Consider the timing of distributions carefully. You may want to consult a qualified tax practitioner.

Why Should You Read This Book?

Aren't magazines and TV news programs designed to help investors make informed decisions? No. They're in business to make money for their owners and advertisers. The media thrives on volatility and uncertainty and they love scandals. Unless you are secure in your knowledge and investment plan, following the media's lead could result in many sleepless nights and bad decisions.

Your 401(k) is vital to your financial future—and the information provided in *Protect Your 401(k)* is vital to understanding your options and what you need to do. *Protect Your 401(k)* will help you manage what may be the most important asset you will ever own.

Notes

1. At the end of 1999, there were 340,000 401(k) plans with 34 million participants. Danny Hakim, "Controlling 401(k) Assets: Fight Brewing over Investment Choices for $1.7 Trillion," *The New York Times*, November 17, 2000.
2. Bob Goodman, Putnam senior economist, phone conversation with me, October 15, 2001.
3. Staff, "Making Your Money Last" (Seeking Advice: Planning Challenge), *Mutual Funds*, March 2002.

1

PAY YOURSELF FIRST

WHILE RETIREMENT MAY SEEM LIKE A distant goal and amassing enough to live on when you don't make a six-figure salary may seem difficult, the sooner you get started, the better your chances of reaching your goals. Just because you may not retire to a villa in the south of France doesn't mean that you can't achieve financial security on your own terms.

For many people in today's workforce, investing in a 401(k) plan is the single best opportunity they have to achieve a financially secure retirement. It's a "get rich slowly" approach that gives you an opportunity, over time, to amass a substantial nest egg for your retirement.

For the first time in 20 years, Congress has vastly expanded the incentive to save. The new tax law, the Economic Growth and Tax Relief Reconciliation Act of 2001, really encourages people to participate in 401(k)s and to do everything they can to take control.

Despite this, nearly a quarter (24%) of the workers who have an opportunity to contribute to a company-sponsored retirement plan do not participate, according to the 2001 *Retirement Confidence Survey* conducted by Hewitt Associates, a global consulting firm. Of those who do contribute, more than half do not contribute enough to earn the maximum possible employer matching contribution.

When asked why they don't participate in the company 401(k) plan, the most common answer from employees is "Because I can't afford to." Frankly, this answer couldn't be more wrong. The fact is *you can't afford not to!*

> **The steps you take now will lay the groundwork for the lifestyle you will enjoy when you retire.**

The future is coming. When it gets here, you want to be ready. The steps you take now will lay the groundwork for the lifestyle you will enjoy when you retire. If you want to enjoy a future that is free from financial worries, you need to start saving today. Hewitt Associates reports that the average balance in an employer-sponsored retirement plan in the year 2000 was only $52,974. How far would that go in supporting you during retirement?

Pay Yourself First

To achieve long-term financial security, many financial experts recommend budgeting at least 10% of your yearly gross income toward that goal. Unfortunately, for some people who are just beginning to save, 10% is considerably more than they can afford, so they get discouraged and don't save anything. Of those who do save, the average 401(k) plan participant contributes only 6.5% of his or her gross yearly pay to the plan, according to Hewitt Associates.

If you aren't saving anything now, and you're overwhelmed at the thought of a 10% savings rate, start your personal savings program by setting a more realistic goal. Start by contributing just 1% of your gross annual income to your 401(k) plan. To frame this savings goal in terms of real dollars, calculate 1% of your gross yearly income and then divide by 12. If the cash value of 1% is more than you are able to save right now, reduce it by half. Next, designate the proper dollar amount to be withdrawn from your paycheck and your 401(k) will make an automatic investment in your future every time you get paid. While a few dollars every month might not seem like much at first, over the long haul, every little bit adds up.

Initially, the dollar figure involved isn't nearly as important as the fact that you have made a commitment to the "pay yourself first" philosophy. It's all about prioritizing your life so that a financially secure future is your top financial goal. When it comes right down to it, you don't need to have any Wall Street investment expertise to make an

> The dollar figure involved isn't nearly as important as the fact that you have made a commitment to the "pay yourself first" philosophy.

investment in yourself. You simply need to keep in mind that an investment in yourself is the most important investment you can make.

By dedicating a percentage of your income toward saving for the future, you have made a conscious decision that your future is important. You have made a commitment that an investment in yourself comes before your membership at the health club, a day at the spa, or a night on the town with dinner and dancing. You have made a decision that saving for the future is more important than spending money on recreation today.

When your financial situation improves and circumstances permit, gradually increase the amount of money earmarked for your 401(k) plan and your savings will hit that 10% mark more quickly than you might think. Once you get to 10%, there's no reason to stop there. If you can afford to increase your contribution percentage beyond 10%, you may be able to retire early. If you choose to keep working to full retirement age, your 401(k) balance will be that much better off for every extra dollar that you saved. Rest assured that when you're relaxing on the beach somewhere 20 years from now, you won't be complaining that you have too much money in your 401(k) plan.

Now, the next step is to reduce your expenses and, thereby, increase the amount of money you have available to invest.

Sweat the Small Stuff!

If you're like most people, you tend to think about money in a grand sense. You view your personal finances on a macro scale (the cost of a house, the cost of a car, the cost of an expensive vacation) instead of on a micro scale (the price of lunch, the cost of a pack of cigarettes). This is a bad habit, because in planning for the big stuff, you overlook total cost of all the little items that nibble away at your pocketbook everyday.

While most Americans are overextended on their mortgage and drive a car they can't really afford, these major expenses, despite the enormous drag on finances that they represent, aren't what keeps us living paycheck to paycheck. It's the small stuff. That $1.50 per day spent on coffee, the $5.50 on lunch, and the $3.50 for a magazine quickly add up to hundreds of dollars a month and thousands of dollars a year. Don't forget about banking and ATM fees. Pay attention to those fees and avoid them whenever possible.

While a few dollars a day might seem insignificant in light of your mortgage or car payments, just $2 a day adds up to $744 per year. If you can save just $10 a week from your grocery bill and put it in your 401(k) plan instead, you've just found another $520. Add that to the daily cost of a fast-food lunch, and you've got several thousand dollars that can go into your 401(k) this year, and the year after.

That's it. No magic tricks, no get-rich-quick schemes. Just live within your means. To make this happen, you need to review your finances, put together a prudent financial plan, and stick to it.

The Budget

For some people, just the mention of the word "budget" conjures up images of spending limitations and being unable to afford life's little (and big!) luxuries. This self-defeating image couldn't be further from the truth. Yes, it is true that careful management of your finances may stop you from making purchases that you can't truly afford and racking up big debts, but the real truth about budgeting is something that most consumers simply overlook. *Budgets are a tool for growth!*

Every successful company in the country, from General Electric and Wal-Mart to the local restaurant and the corner gas station, has a budget. The companies that operate within their budgets succeed. Those that do not, fail. Now, putting that in terms of your personal life, think about yourself as the CEO of your future. Your life is a business that you run. You have income and you have expenses. You have long-term goals and short-term needs. If you plan well and stick to your budget, you will significantly increase your chances of success. Unsuccessful investors don't plan to fail; they just fail to plan.

Budgeting does not require fancy spreadsheets or expensive software. It begins with a humble pencil and paper. For one week, carry a pencil and paper with you and keep track of how much money you spend. Write it all down—not just every dime, every penny. Whether you spend 60 cents for a donut or $11.23 for groceries, write it down.

> Budgeting does not require fancy spreadsheets or expensive software. It begins with a humble pencil and paper.

At the end of the week, take out your piece of paper and add up the numbers. You'll be amazed at where all of your money has gone. If you take a good look at that list, you're likely to notice that you spent a significant amount of money on items that you didn't need and/or you'd be willing to do without. When you add up the numbers, you will truly develop a newfound awareness of how extraneous purchases drain away your hard-earned dollars.

To truly take control of your future, you need to take a close look at your lifestyle.

Do you really need a cell phone? How about that pager? Generations of families survived without pagers. Is your monthly long-distance telephone bill out of control? Do you spend too much money on fast food? How much is that cable bill? How about those magazine subscriptions? Do you clip coupons? Do you look at the price on the sign in front of the gas station before you pull in and fill up? Is the cost of that membership in the gym really worth it? Do you need to drive a gas-guzzling sport utility vehicle just to get to and from work?

It is quite likely that more than a few of your monthly expenses could be eliminated without making any detrimental changes to your lifestyle. Certainly, you have to strike a balance between enjoying your life today and saving for tomorrow, but a little prudence can go a long way.

Debra Pankow, Family Economics Specialist at North Dakota State University, compiled the data in Figure 1-1 for household expenditures for the average U.S. consumer unit (families, households, or individuals) for 1998. Since inflation has been virtually flat since then, the data should still be pretty close to the mark.

While everyone has different needs, interests, and expenses, generally speaking, you would do well to spend less than the average in every category except "Pension." (Think of "Pension" as your 401(k) plan and other retirement investments.)

Credit cards are a consumer's worst nightmare. Next to house payments and car payments, monthly credit card payments account for the next most significant chunk of monthly expenses for many consumers. The high credit allowances that most cards offer are designed to convince consumers to rack up mountains of debt that will take years to pay off.

According to American Consumer Credit Counseling, Inc., a consumer with an $8,000 credit card balance making the minimum monthly payment at 18% interest will pay $15,432 in interest and take 25

FIGURE 1-1   Household expenses chart.

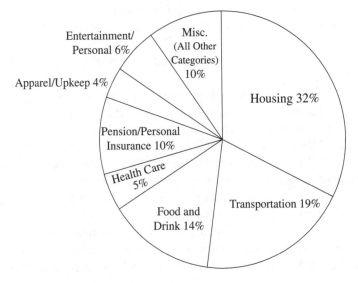

years, 7 months to pay off the debt. That $8,000 purchase will cost you $23,432 by the time your balance is paid off. For the credit card companies, it's a great strategy that has paid big dividends.

Make a commitment to stop using your credit cards unless you already have the money to pay for your purchases in cash, but don't happen to have the cash with you at the moment. This way, you never buy anything that you can't afford and you never pay interest. Ideally, don't have more than two credit cards. The more cards you have, the more likely you are to use them.

Then, identify the cards charging the highest interest rates and pay them off first. If you can't afford to pay off the balances all at once, start by making a commitment to send in more than just the minimum required monthly payment. In the meantime, if you can get a lower interest rate by consolidating your credit card debt onto a single card, do it.

When You "Find" More Money, Invest It!

Once you've done everything you can do to live within your means, and hopefully well below, you need to remain constantly on the lookout for additional opportunities to increase the amount you save in your 401(k). Anytime you get a raise or earn a bonus is a prime opportunity to increase your savings. Since you were able to get by on your former salary, the additional income is "found" money. Adding this money to your monthly investment should be completely painless.

Perhaps the most important fact to keep in mind is that *knowledge may be power, but action is everything!*

2

INCREASE YOUR CONTRIBUTIONS

The 401(k) is the favorite tax-deferred investment vehicle of upper management!

SAY YOU'RE ONE OF THOSE PEOPLE WHO IS not convinced that a substantial portion of your paycheck should be dedicated to your 401(k) plan. There is something that you should know! In executive suites across corporate America, highly paid corporate leaders are on the lookout for ways to increase participation in the company 401(k) plan. They want to get employees contributing at the highest possible deferral rate and keep them contributing for as long as possible.

Why? Hey, it's not because they want to ensure that you have a financially secure retirement. Sure, if you do participate in the plan, you are more likely to reach your long-term retirement goals; but if *you* don't participate, the executives won't be able to sock away their own maximum contribution amount in their 401(k) plans. That's right! The contributions highly compensated employees (people who will earn more than $130,000 in 2002) can make to their 401(k) plans are directly limited by the amount of money contributed by everybody else who works for the company. So, the more they can get you to save, the more they can save!

And why should this matter to you? Think about it. The highest-paid people in the country believe that 401(k) plans are such a good investment vehicle that they are willing to give other employees money (matched contributions) to participate in their 401(k) plans so that they can maximize their own contributions. The average worker can

> The highest-paid people in the country believe that 401(k) plans are such a good investment vehicle that they are willing to give other employees money to participate.

share in an investment that is a priority in the executive's retirement portfolio. That fact alone should be a compelling reason for every eligible corporate employee in the country to contribute the maximum possible amount they can afford without starving to death or sending their children to school barefoot.

Eligibility (Who Can Invest?)

Previously, employers made you wait a year or required that you be 21—or both—before you could be eligible to participate in their retirement plans. This was primarily to lessen the impact of turnover, which occurs most frequently within the first year of employment. Now, about 75% of all 401(k) plans have no tenure or age restriction.

In fact, a trend you're likely to see at your employer is *automatic enrollment,* meaning that you are automatically enrolled in the 401(k) plan, usually within the first 45 days of employment and typically at about 3% of pay, which is invested in either a money market or a balanced-fund option in your plan. Automatic enrollment has become very popular, especially among employers that have historically had poor participation (such as retailers, nonprofits, and low-wage manufacturing).

Plus, there is no longer a limit of 25% of your salary when funding a 401(k) plan. Now even part-time or low-income earners can contribute the full $11,000-$15,000 if they can swing it.

However, for those plans that haven't been updated, the old rules and definitions still apply. The 401(k) plan may require the employee to complete up to one *year of service* to become eligible to participate in the plan. The plan may also impose a requirement that the employee be 21 years of age or older.

A *year of service* is calculated generally as a 12-month period, beginning on the first day of employment, during which an employee completes at least 1,000 hours of service. If the employee does not complete 1,000 hours of service during the initial eligibility computation period, the next period begins on the anniversary date of employment or, if provided in the plan, on the first day of the plan year during which the anniversary date falls. Years of service with a previous employer can qualify for eligibility and vesting if the successor employer maintains the previous employer's qualified plan.

An *hour of service* includes periods of time such as vacations, holidays, illness, jury duty, and other specified instances during which no real work was performed but the employee nonetheless received compensation.

It's to the employee's benefit to make sure their company's 401(k) plan has been brought up to the new tax rules. Check with your plan sponsor on the status.

Elective Contributions of Pre-Tax Dollars

All 401(k) plans by definition permit CODAs. The term CODA (cash or deferred arrangement) refers precisely to the ability of eligible employees to elect a *contribution rate,* also known as deferral percentage or savings rate, up to an allowable maximum percentage of their *pre-tax* compensation, to be contributed to the plan by the employer on the employee's behalf. The amount contributed to the plan under the CODA is called an *elective contribution.*

These elective contributions and the earnings on those contributions are not subject to income taxes, federal or state (except in Pennsylvania), until you withdraw those funds. A 10% penalty tax is imposed if you withdraw the funds prior to age 59½.

Your contributions will be deducted from your paycheck every pay period. For example, if you gross $3,000 per month and you've select-ed a 10% contribution rate, you're putting $300 a month ($3,000 x 10% = $300) into your 401(k) account. Most companies track the amount that you have contributed on your paycheck. You can usually change your contribution rate on a daily, monthly, or quarterly basis.

Recently enacted changes in laws governing 401(k) plans provide dramatically higher contribution limits and even catch-up options that can make up for poor savings habits or to simply maximize tax defer-ral and wealth accumulation. In 2001, the maximum annual contribution level for 401(k) plans was $10,500. This limit is increased to $11,000 for the 2002 tax year and will continue to increase at the rate of $1,000 per year through the year 2006, when it will be $15,000.

> **Recently enacted changes in laws governing 401(k) plans provide dramatically higher contribution limits and even catch-up options that can make up for poor savings habits**

Beyond 2006, further increases will be based on the inflation rate, as computed by the federal government. In addition, if you are 50 years of age or older, you can make a graduated *catch-up* contribution of $1,000 beginning in the tax year 2002, increasing in increments of $1000 per year, up to $5000 in 2006. So, in 2003, the catch-up provision allows an extra contribution of $2000, in 2004, it's $3000 and in 2005, it's $4,000.

Exponential Growth Through Compounding

The acceleration of wealth accumulation through compounding is a major selling point for participating in a 401(k). That is, you earn on the cumulative of your *contributions* AND your *tax savings* AND on the *earnings* on your investments.

Figure 2-1 will show you how much you'd need to contribute monthly, the number of years until retirement, and the rates of return you'd need to have a million dollars at retirement. It's not impossible!

FIGURE 2-1   Amounts and time required to save a million dollars
(from *The First Time Investor's Workbook*, McGraw-Hill, 2001).

| | | \multicolumn{6}{c}{Number of Years Until Retirement} | | | | |
		15 Yrs	20 Yrs	25 Yrs	30 Yrs	35 Yrs	40 Yrs
	$25	64%	36%	28%	22%	19%	16%
	$50	45%	32%	24%	19%	16%	14%
	$100	39%	28%	21%	17%	14%	11%
Monthly Contribution	$250	31%	22%	16%	13%	10%	8%
	$500	25%	17%	12%	9%	7%	6%
	$1K	19%	12%	8%	6%	4%	3%
	$2K	12%	7%	4%	2%	1%	0.2%

A Savings Regimen (or Dollar Cost Averaging)

Elective contributions to your 401(k) through payroll deduction become automatic dollar cost average investing. It eliminates the worry of "should I or shouldn't I?" 401(k) investors have no reason to fear market declines. The dollar cost averaging 401(k) plan investor begins to almost wait in anticipation of the next mini-crash, instead of dreading it. Why? Because it can help you turn the characteristic fluctuations of mutual fund values into a benefit, because you are investing over different time periods.

Dollar Cost Averaging

More simply put: when mutual fund prices are low, you're able to purchase more fund shares, and when prices go back up, you'll be purchasing fewer shares. Ideally, while you are in your accumulation years, you'll want the market to remain low. This way you'll end up with more shares. As the years roll along and the stock market continues to go up in value, your shares do, too (Figure 2-2).

When you think about this, you won't be so worried when the market is down—especially if it's around the time you are buying more shares. The game here is to purchase shares at an average cost that is below the average price.

FIGURE 2-2 Dollar cost averaging.

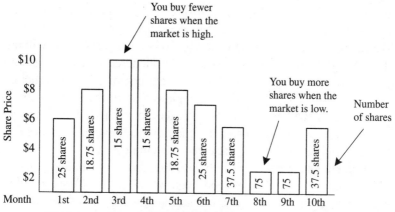

- Total amount invested: $1,500 ($150/month)
- Average price of these 10 purchases: $6.00
- Average cost per share: $4.38
- Total shares: 342.50
- Average cost per share: $150/month times 10 months =
  $1,500 divided by 342.50 (total shares) = $4.38 average cost

After-Tax Contributions

Most 401(k) plans permit employees to make additional contributions beyond the pre-tax limits using after-tax dollars. These after-tax dollars would generate earnings tax-free until they are withdrawn. When such an option is available in the plan, the plan cannot condition the right to make such after-tax contributions on an employee's participation in the pre-tax CODA.

Retirement Plan Contribution Options

Participation Incentives: These expanded contribution limits are great news, but when 20% to 25% of eligible workers are *not* participating, and those who do participate make only *minimum* contributions, there must be a bigger issue. Although the tax-deferral point is attractive, many people don't feel comfortable investing in a 401(k) because it ties up access to their money and/or they don't feel confident about their job security. Another major reason among the rank-and-file employees for not participating is that they need as much from their paycheck as they can get.

Indeed, participation in 401(k) plans varies dramatically by salary range. Hewitt Associates reports that only 43% of workers earning less than $20,000 participate in their 401(k) plan, while workers earning $40,000 or more have an average participation rate that exceeds 76%. Because of these participation rates, half of 401(k) plans (47%) will fail the non-discrimination tests when deferral percentage participation rates of highly compensated employees are compared with participation rates of other employees. These plans, due to the Department of Labor's rules, will be forced to limit the percentage of income that highly compensated executives can contribute to their 401(k) plans due to low participation rates by rank-and-file employees.

If you made less than $85,000 in 2001, this means nothing to you. But if you made $85,000 or more, you would be considered a highly compensated employee and your contributions may be limited to 4%, 6%, 8%, or 10% of your pay, far below the allowable contribution maximum. Permitting these employees to make after-tax contributions is one way to lessen the impact of a cap.

Sources of Contributions

To get employee participation rates higher, many companies offer to match their employees' contributions within their 401(k) plans. In fact, Hewitt Associates reports that 72% of the companies with 401(k) plans offer matching contributions.

In most plans, however, the companies will only offer to match employees' pre-tax contributions, but you should check your summary plan description to see if your company will match your after-tax contributions as well. In some cases, companies in order to increase participation levels, will make contributions for all employees, even those not personally contributing themselves, but this is rare. As an incentive to keep employees participating on a long-term basis, the Hewitt survey reveals that 67% of employers have set up vesting schedules that require employees to participate in the plan for a certain number of years before employees get full ownership of the company's matching contribution (Figures 2-3 and 2-4).

FIGURE 2-3 Employee contributions.

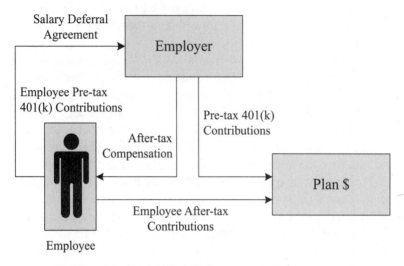

FIGURE 2-4 401(k) plan sources of contributions.

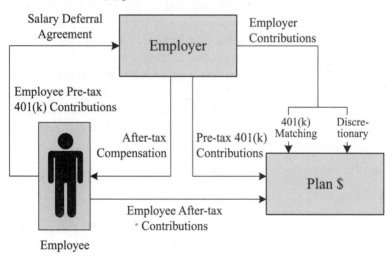

Not Just for Retirement

The 401(k) is not just a retirement savings vehicle: using the after-tax contribution feature of a 401(k) plan to achieve your other financial goals may make sense. After-tax contributions provide you with the opportunity to save for a goal and withdraw the money without having to take a loan from your 401(k). You can't borrow your after-tax contributions (take a loan), but you *can* withdraw them and you won't have to pay the 10% penalty tax.

However, the IRS says when you withdraw even a dollar of your after-tax contributions, a portion of the money you get back may be investment earnings. If that's the case, as a result, you'll get hit with 20% withholding (unless it's a hardship withdrawal) and a 10% penalty tax on the *earnings portion only*. Think about after-tax contributions to your 401(k) plan this way: it's an insurance policy to protect you in case you need the money, without the necessity of having to repay it.

The new law also enhances portability, or transferability, of retirement accounts beginning in the 2002 tax year. It simplifies rollovers and encourages employers to use faster vesting schedules for matching contributions. Also, when you change jobs, direct rollovers of after-tax contributions to 401(k)s will be allowed either to a traditional IRA or to your new employer's defined-contribution plan. This greatly simplifies the process, which formerly required a separate check to be cut for the after-tax amount. But, make sure you track your "already-been-taxed" contributions apart from your "never-been-taxed" contributions and earnings (use an IRS Form 8606 for this chore). If you don't track this, the IRS could fine you and tax your already-taxed money. To avoid this, be sure you instruct the record keeper to roll over the investment earnings position to an IRA as a trustee-to-trustee transfer of this money. Figure 2-5 summarizes the 401(k) process as it generally practiced in most organizations.

FIGURE 2-5   The 401(k) process.

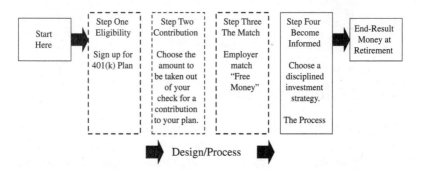

Using Both a 401(k) and an IRA Makes Sense

Since there are new types of IRAs available, it might appear that they could replace your 401(k). But, before you make any major decisions, understand all the facts:

- **Deductible IRA vs. 401(k)?** A tax deduction on an IRA will generally have less of an effect than a pre-tax 401(k) deduction, because a 401(k) gives you the tax savings with each paycheck. With an IRA, you have to wait until you file your taxes to get the tax benefit. Meanwhile, your 401(k) tax savings has been earning all year long. In addition, you cannot borrow money from your IRA for long periods of time. But, if you're a highly compensated employee and your 401(k) pre-tax and after-tax contributions are limited (capped), you can still take advantage of the expanded contribution limits of an IRA for you and your spouse. Even if you are not eligible for a tax deduction, an IRA still provides an additional retirement savings opportunity.
- **Roth IRA vs. 401(k)?** Using a Roth IRA means that you are betting that your tax rate in retirement will be equal to or higher than your current rate. (That is, you're counting on paying less in taxes now on the money that you put into a Roth IRA than you would pay on your 401(k) money after you retire.) Consider first maximizing your contribution to a Roth IRA before making after-tax contributions to your 401(k). Earnings on your after-tax contributions to a 401(k) are taxed at regular income tax rates at retirement. Roth IRA's earnings are tax-free after age 59½, and you can withdraw your contributions at any time without paying income or penalty taxes.
- **Ed IRA vs. 401(k)?** The value of an Educational IRA is its tax-free feature, its higher income limits for married couples, and the flexibility to use these monies for expenses of education, public or private, kindergarten through graduate school. If the purpose of your savings is for education, an Ed IRA would beat the 401(k) plan. But an even better choice might be a Section 529 plan, also known as a "qualified state tuition program." There are two types of 529 plans, *prepaid tuition* and *savings*

account, in which you can save more (up to $50,000 per year per beneficiary) and have investment flexibility. Some states even offer a state income tax deduction. Go to **www.savingfor-college.com** or **www.money.com** for more information on these plans.

If Ed IRAs and Section 529 plans aren't enough, The Economic Growth and Tax Relief Reconciliation Act of 2001 also provides a tax deduction for college tuition and a deduction for student loan interest. If you're considering using your home equity to pay college expenses, the double deduction could produce a very inexpensive loan.

The last word on the subject is this: stay with your 401(k) until you have maxed out your yearly plan limit or tax-deferral limit, as well as any catch-up contributions!

3

TAKE FULL ADVANTAGE OF MATCHING CONTRIBUTIONS

Every time there is an employer match, it is a guaranteed 100% return on your money.

DON'T TURN DOWN FREE MONEY! That's what you're doing if your company offers a 401(k) or similar retirement savings plan with an employer match and you're not participating to the fullest. Most employers will match a certain percentage of the workers' contributions to the 401(k) plan, because it's a way to further compensate, encourage, and retain key employees and the employer gets a tax deduction by doing so. Just like the contributions out of your own pocket, the employer's contributions almost always go into the account as pre-tax dollars. This means the money is not taxed until it's withdrawn, so it's earning and compounding free of current taxation. You would be crazy to not get as much of this money as you are eligible for!

FIGURE 3-1   Increased match results.

Many plan sponsors offer
different matches. A typical
arrangement is a 50% match,
and more employers are
offering 100% matches or
higher. Push for higher match.

In this example our employee
is 40 years old. She makes
$90,000 annually, has 4%
increases, and has saved
$100,000.

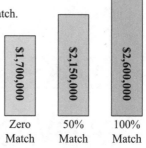

A 100% match results in nearly a millon dollars more in
retirement than employees who receive no match.

According to the Employee Benefit Research Institute's 2000
Survey of Defined Contribution Plans, about 84% of companies that
provide 401(k) plans also offer to match their employees' contributions
at some percentage. The most common match is 50 cents on each dollar the employee contributes, up to a maximum of 6% of that employee's compensation. This 3% match rate (50% of 6% = 3%) is found in
almost 35% of 401(k) plans, but a fair number of employers offer
matches of 100% or even higher. That means when you put in a dollar,
so do they.

Read Your Plan's Fine Print

Since these matched contributions are appearing more as part of the
overall compensation package, the 401(k) plan's design is critical to
maximize the value of a company's human resource dollar. Take the
time to study your company's summary plan description (SPD). See if
it specifies that your company's 401(k) has a *nondiscretionary* match;
that means that the plan sponsor *must* make a contribution. Even if your
plan's match is *discretionary* (only about 20% of 401(k) plans have a

discretionary match), the company still probably offers a matched contribution. Discretionary matches are usually based upon the company being profitable.

Also, it's to your benefit to check out the definition of *compensation* in your SPD to determine the types of pay that will be matched. Regular pay, such as salary or hourly pay plus overtime, are the most common definitions. But compensation could also include commissions, bonuses, shift differentials, or special

> The more often matched money is added, the greater the benefit of compounding to you.

awards. Since matched funds have a ceiling of a specified percentage of your compensation, you want to be sure you're using the highest total in your computation. Increase your contribution accordingly to receive the full benefit of any matched money.

Learn how often and when matched money is deposited into your account. The more often matched money is added, the greater the benefit of compounding to you. Many plans match your account only if you're still employed on specific dates—say, December 31, the last day of the year. You won't consider yourself very smart if you leave the company on December 29, only to find out that you were two days short of receiving the next quarterly, semiannual, or annual match contribution.

Any money that *you* put into a 401(k) is always 100% *vested* (yours to take) immediately, though it will then be subject to taxes and maybe a penalty. But, about 70% of all 401(k) plans have some type of vesting requirement on any matched money contributions. Vesting schedules require an employee to remain employed by the sponsor and participate in the plan for a certain period of time in order to own 100% of the employer's contributions. However, most vesting schedules have been dramatically shortened, which means that you could change employers sooner and keep all or a great percentage of your accumulated matched contributions.

The vesting clock starts ticking whether or not you are enrolled in the plan. In applying these vesting rules, know how your company's plan defines a *year of service*, which can be a calendar year, a plan year, or any period consisting of 12 consecutive months during which the participant has completed 1,000 or more hours of service. Internal

Revenue Code section 411 specifies permissible vesting schedules that establish limits on the amount of time that a plan may require an employee to vest in his or her benefits.

The two most common types of vesting are *graded* vesting and *cliff* vesting.

Graded vesting. You own an increasing portion of any matched money contribution each year that you are employed with the company. If you are participating in a four-year graded plan, you vest or own 25% of the company money every year (25% x 4 years = 100%). In a five-year graded plan, you own 20% per year. If you leave your employment before you are fully vested, you are entitled to the current vesting percentage of the matched monies.

A graded vesting schedule cannot exceed six years. If you work for the government, then the minimum that you can vest is 20% after two years, 40% after three years, 60% after four years, and 80% after five years, with 100% vesting at six years. Table 3-1 shows an example of four years of graded vesting.

Years of Service	Cumulative % Earned
1	25%
2	50%
3	75%
4	100%

TABLE 3-1   Example of four-year graded vesting.

Cliff vesting. You own nothing until a certain period of time has passed. If you leave before you are fully vested, you get nothing. As you can see, there is a big incentive to hang in there until you are vested. Cliff vesting is most common in defined benefit plans, but you will also find it in about 13% of 401(k) plans. Employers who use cliff vesting are required to vest you 100% after your third year of service. Table 3-2 shows an example of three-year cliff vesting.

A match in the form of company stock is *not* necessarily a bad thing. In many of the large plans, all or part of the employer's matched contribution is in the form of company stock, so the employer doesn't have

Years of Service	Cumulative % Earned
1	0%
2	0%
3	100%

TABLE 3-2   Example of three-year cliff vesting.

to expend cash or take the contributions as an expense on the company's income statement. The belief is that employees who owns shares in their employer have a certain pride of ownership or interest in the company's well-being and it demonstrates management's good faith in the company's future.

The bull market of the past 20 years masked the problems associated with owning company stock inside your 401(k) plan. As long as the market was going up, most companies' stocks soared in value along with 401(k) account balances, and employees were happy to get free shares of company stock contributed to their long-term

> The bull market of the past 20 years masked the problems associated with owning company stock inside your 401(k) plan.

retirement plan. Whether out of loyalty, ignorance, or convenience, more and more employees opted to direct all or a large percentage of their own contributions to be also invested in company stock. According to the Profit-Sharing/401(k) Council of America, the single largest investment in 401(k) plans is employer's stock—39% of total assets. This high percentage of concentration and overweighting in a single equity resulted in an imprudent exposure to volatility and business risk.

When, in 2001, many publicly held companies dropped 40% to 60% of their value, those 401(k) portfolios that weren't diversified over different asset classes suffered terrifying losses. Unlike defined benefit or pension plans, 401(k) contribution plans are *not* required by law to *diversify* their holdings—although there is now a rush to do that.

What happened at Enron is a glaring example of overweighting in one stock. About 63% of the employees' retirement money was invested in Enron stock. When Enron imploded, some $1 billion of savings disappeared. Now everyone is scrutinizing their portfolios to see if they are overweight in one company and, to the extent they are, they're going to be shuffling assets around to reduce that exposure.

Of course, there are always two sides to every story. On one side of this issue are situations like the downfall of Enron, Global Crossing, or Lucent Technology. On the opposite side are the companies such as General Electric, Dell, Wal-Mart, Home Depot, and Microsoft, whose value is up hundreds, if not thousands, of percent over the last 10 years. For instance, $10,000 of Microsoft stock acquired in 1986 would be worth $5 million today!

We spoke to Keith Clark of DWC Consultants, who has over 16 years of employee benefits consulting experience. He said, "For every negative story related to company stock, I can tell you a good one. There's nothing wrong with owning company stock, as long as you accept the volatility issue and you have the time to make up losses. Company stock is a risk and it should be communicated as such."

Company Stock and Your Job

Most employees don't understand that what they're doing is placing a whopper of a bet on their employer when their primary income depends on the company, their benefits depend on it, and all their 401(k) assets also depend on the value of its stock. The future security and value of each of these is tied together. Many of the companies whose shares have dropped 50% in value over the last 12 months have also down-sized. So, not only did some participants lose significant value in their retirement plans, many lost their income and benefits, as well.

In order to recover from a 50% loss, a 100% gain needs to occur. And, that's possible over time. But, if you're 59 years old and planning to retire and 60% of your 401(k) plan assets were in Enron, you're sunk. You don't have the time to make up for losses that you sustained. Table 3-3 shows the amount of time you'll need to break even under various scenarios.

The way to correct an overweighting in company stock is to diversify a percentage of your 401(k) assets into some other investment that

If You Lose This Much ...	... You'll Need to Earn This Much to Break Even
10%	11%
20%	25%
30%	43%
40%	67%
50%	100%
60%	150%
70%	233%
80%	400%
90%	900%

TABLE 3-3   Regaining your loss.

tends to move dissimilarly to your company stock. This may seem like common sense, but, in fact, it was a dramatic breakthrough in investment methodology when Harry Markowitz developed the Nobel Prize-winning theory back in the 1950s.

Markowitz demonstrated that, to the extent that securities in a portfolio do *not* move in concert with each other, their individual risks could be effectively diversified away. We address this in more detail in Chapter 4, but there's a great practical explanation of how effective diversification works in Burton Malkiel's book, *A Random Walk Down Wall Street*,[1] that we paraphrase as follows:

	Umbrella Manufacturer	Resort Owner
Rainy Season	+50	–25
Sunny Season	–25	+50

Let's suppose we have an island economy with only two businesses. The first is a beach resort and the second is a manufacturer of umbrellas. Weather affects the fortunes of both. During sunny seasons, the resort does a booming business, but umbrella sales plummet.

During rainy seasons, the resort owner does poorly, while the umbrella manufacturer is making money.

The following is a hypothetical comparison of the earnings of the two businesses during different seasons:

Suppose that, on average, half the seasons are sunny and half are rainy (i.e., the probability of a sunny or rainy season is 50/50). Let's make this simple and say our investor had $2 to invest and, instead of putting all his money into one business or the other, the investor diversified and put half his money into the umbrella manufacturer and half into the resort business. In the sunny seasons, his $1 investment in the resort produces a 50-cent return, while a $1 investment in umbrella manufacturing would lose 25 cents. During the rainy seasons, the exact opposite would happen: the investment in the umbrella company produces a good 50% return, while the investment in the resort loses 25%. The investor would never earn less than a return of 12½%, or 25 cents on his $2 investment.

None of the foregoing is to suggest that you should turn down a matched contribution just because it's in the form of company stock. It's just that you should view your investment in your company stock as a *part* of your 40l(k), not the whole thing. That's still free money and, even if it became worthless, there's no cost to you. You still have your elected contributions, hopefully, diversified in other investments.

If you leave your company and you have shares of company stock in your 401(k) plan, you can either transfer the stock to an IRA or new 40l(k) plan, or take the stock now. If you take the stock now, you will pay ordinary income tax on the stock's basis (what it cost you to buy it, not its appreciated value). The new capital gains tax rates often make it better to pay ordinary income tax on your stock's basis now and sell it later, when you will be taxed at a 20% rate (or 18%, if you hold it for five years). This beats paying an income tax rate of 27%, 30%, 35%, or 38.6% down the road. (Income rates will drop every two years until 2006.) If you elect to not take the stock, there will be no tax now, but you will pay ordinary tax on the full value of the stock when it is later distributed.

Now, here are a few *Enron-proof* rules to keep in mind regarding company stock inside your 401(k):

- If you have the option to choose between a matching contribution of stock or cash, choose cash—for its liquidity as well as your ability to direct its investment. (Remember: you are already betting your wages on the future of your employer, and you may also be participating in their stock option plan!)
- If you do have company stock, don't exceed 10% ownership of company stock inside your plan.
- If your plan sponsor requires that company stock must be held for a certain period, even after it is fully vested inside the plan, *rebalance* your percentage of stock ownership in your overall 401(k) as soon as possible.
- Evaluate your company stock as objectively as any other type of investment.
- Evaluate your tax options concerning company stock if you leave your employer—whether you change jobs or retire.

Note

1. Malkiel, Burton G. *A Random Walk Down Wall Street*. 1999. New York: W.W. Norton & Company, Inc.

C H A P T E R

KNOW HOW
YOUR PLAN
WORKS

IT'S IMPORTANT TO UNDERSTAND THE BASIC mechanics of
how your 401(k) plan works and how to use it to your advantage.

A Definition

Technically, a 401(k) plan is a defined contribution retirement plan that
allows workers to save for retirement in accounts invested in equities,
fixed-income securities, and bonds. The contributions are made before
tax and any earnings on those contributions compound tax-free until
distribution in retirement. The plan is sponsored by firms for their
employees and, in recent years, these accounts have grown with such
speed and popularity that they are displacing traditional defined benefit pension plans.[1]

Your company may offer a SIMPLE (Savings Incentive Match Plan
for Employees) plan. Started in 1997, SIMPLE plans are intended for
companies with fewer than 100 employees. They operate the same as
regular 401(k)s, but with much less paperwork. However, they require
the company to contribute to an employee's account.

The 401(k) Plan's Fiduciaries

Fiduciaries are people responsible for making decisions about how a 401(k) plan operates. Most fiduciaries work for the company but must perform their duties on behalf of the plan's participants and their beneficiaries. Fiduciaries cannot make decisions that would be considered careless, foolhardy, or lacking in intelligence. Their guiding light is the common-law principle known as the *prudent investor rule*.

Definitions

Plan sponsor This is the owner. The sponsor has to want to play the 401(k) game. In almost all cases, it will be your employer. The sponsor designs the plan and makes the rules that employees must follow. The sponsor also hires the rest of the key personnel that a 401(k) plan needs to operate.

Plan trustee This is the security guard, the person who holds onto your money and makes sure that no one can get to it.

Plan administrator This is the manager. The administrator is responsible for the day-to-day administration of your 401(k) plan. The manager can usually be found at your company in your benefits or finance department.

Record keeper This is the umpire, who is always keeping score. The record keeper keeps track of your account, whether you're buying or selling, borrowing or withdrawing, coming or going. The record keeper will also send a scorecard each quarter, or at least each year, to tell you how you're doing—and if you're winning or losing.

Investment manager This is your agent. The *plan sponsor* is responsible for hiring and firing agents, not *you*. Rarely do agents work directly for the owner.

Plan document Every 401(k) has a plan document that tells how it operates. It's very detailed and contains legal information about the 401(k).

Summary plan description (SPD) The law also requires that a summary of the plan document be provided to employees—this is the summary plan description. All the features of your 401(k)—eligibility, benefits, rules, investments, and so on—are laid out in this document in a way that anyone can understand. The Employee Retirement Income Security Act of 1974 (ERISA) requires that you be given a copy no later than 90 days after becoming a participant in the plan.

FIGURE 4-1 401(k) plan components.

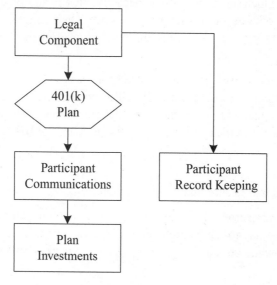

The Process

The 401(k) contribution process begins with the payroll department. The payroll department generally reports year-to-date amounts along with the current deductions from your gross wages on your pay stubs. This is a convenient way to track how frequently and how much you are contributing to your 401(k).

The plan sponsor (employer) has a legal obligation to make sure your 401(k) plan operates according to the law. This means that he or she cannot take money out of your paycheck and leave town with it. In 1997, the U.S. Department of Labor changed the rules to mandate that your employer must forward your 401(k) contributions to the trustee to be invested no later than 15 business days after the end of the month in which that money comes out of your paycheck.

There are ways to extend this 15-day period for up to 10 additional business days, but the reality is that most companies remit 401(k) money to the plan trustee about every two to three weeks. Employers are supposed to notify their employees if they've been holding onto their money for any reason.

Before your contributions can be deposited in the trust, your employer must perform a number of administrative activities for every employee in the plan, like making sure the right percentage was deducted, calculating any match, in some cases segregating your money to be invested according to your wishes, and making sure there are no IRS or other attachments first in line on your money.

In most cases, the company holds this money in what is called a STIF (short-term investment fund) account. The STIF account is a holding tank, usually at a bank, used for money that is waiting to be invested—like a money market account that pays a short-term rate of interest. If the owner of the STIF account is the employer, then your money is still technically part of your employer's "general assets" and the interest earned on the money stays with the company. But, it can also be, and generally is, credited to participants' accounts on a "pro-rata" basis.

Let's say that your employer goes bankrupt between deducting your contribution and putting it into the trust. Because this money is still technically wages, it can revert back to you. Creditors of the company cannot attach your wages, only assets of the company.

When your money reaches the trust, it becomes safe from any troubles or temptations that might beset your employer.

The trustee then invests this money according to your direction. The trustee is a legal entity, usually a bank, insurance company, or investment firm charged with the responsibility of safeguarding your money. Trustees are required by law to protect your money, invest it according to your instructions, and be responsible for keeping track of the plan's assets as a whole, but the trustee is not the record keeper.

If they're serving as investment managers in addition to trustees, they have a responsibility to manage the funds prudently and distribute the funds and earnings to you or your beneficiaries. Trustees carry liability insurance in case they should break this pledge. If the trustee is an individual, say an officer of your company, then he or she must be bonded (have insurance to cover him or her in case he or she makes a mistake).

With plans that match your contributions with company stock or require that the match be invested in a particular type of investment, even though you have no control over that investment, your employer or the trustee is not liable unless you can prove they have done something wrong.

The trustee exercises no judgment on how *you* elect to invest your 401(k) money. Unless the trustee is also the investment manager, the trustee sends your money to the investment manager, generally within 24 hours of receiving it from the company. The money is invested according to the instructions given to the trustee by the record keeper. Like your employer and the investment manager, the trustee also offers no guarantees on the return you'll get on your money.

> The big question for fiduciaries is deciding who should *manage* your money.

The big question, then, for fiduciaries is deciding who should *manage* your money. Just as the fiduciaries pick the plan administrator, the trustee, and the record keeper, they also pick the investment managers. There are really only about six broad choices of managers and, as you can see, there is not a lot of distinction among them:

- **Institutional investment managers.** They set up private accounts and create investment strategies exclusively for your 401(k) plan.
- **Institutional investment advisors.** They set up investment strategies for protective shells such as 401(k), pension, and profit-sharing plans. These investments are not sold to the public, but your 401(k) account balances may be commingled with money from 401(k) participants at other companies.
- **Mutual funds managers.** Your investments are commingled with funds from other 401(k) investors and could also include investments that may be available to the general public.
- **Banks and trust companies.** They generally sell their own investments, but sometimes sell investments for other financial services companies.
- **Insurance companies.** They package their own investments as well as resell other firms' investments.
- **Stockbrokers.** The big brokerage firms (full-service and some discount) usually offer some investment management expertise and maybe an exclusive product, but also resell other firms' investments.

Self-directed brokerage accounts within 401(k) plans are becoming more common, because they allow you to do just what the name implies—invest your hard-earned 401(k) money in almost any stock, bond, or mutual fund that can be traded.

Valuation

How frequently the record keeper performs the reconciliation of your account is called *valuation frequency*. Valuations can be performed daily, monthly, quarterly, semiannually, or annually. You can transact business only as frequently as your account is valued. Today, almost all 401(k) plans are valued daily.

Most likely the record keeper posts your changes at the end of the business day. In other words, if you requested a buy or sell on any given day, you would get that day's price as of the market's close, usually around 4:00 p.m. (EST). Sometimes the buy or sell happens two or three days later, particularly if there are different fund families.

Liquidation

If your plan is terminated by your employer or you leave the company, you have three options:

- Roll your money into the replacement 401(k) plan, if there is one.
- Roll your money into an IRA.
- Cash out of the 401(k).

With the first two options, you'll pay no taxes. If you choose to cash out, set some money aside for taxes, and possibly penalties. Of course, if you have a loan outstanding against your plan when this happens, be sure to first repay it before it goes into default (about 90 days) or it will be treated as a distribution subject to taxes and potential penalties.

> If your company is bought by or merged with another company that has its own 401(k) plan, all your 401(k) money, including loans, will eventually be transferred over to the new plan.

If your company is bought by or merged with another company that has its own 401(k) plan, all your 401(k) money, including loans, will eventually be transferred over to the new plan. This will take three to six months.

If the plan is not terminated, but you leave your employer, you have the same three options. The only way to avoid penalties upon withdrawal before age 59½ is if the plan assets are distributed on account of death or disability.

Legal Protection

The IRS regulations governing 401(k) plans exist to ensure that the plan operates fairly with respect to all employees and not in any way that would discriminate in favor of highly compensated employees to the detriment of the rank-and-file employees. To reach this result, the 401(k) regulations impose a multitude of tests generally designed to maintain an IRS-acceptable balance among all classes of employees in the extent to which they participate and benefit under the plan.

While the U.S. Department of Labor has the authority and responsibility through the Employee Retirement Income Security Act of 1974 (ERISA) to govern the prudent investment management of qualified plan assets, there are no guarantees that your money is safe when it's invested. Although your money is generally safe from the investment manager going bankrupt or committing a criminal offense, there is no insurance against actual investment risk.

> The IRS regulations governing 401(k) plans exist to ensure that the plan operates fairly with respect to all employees

ERISA is the employee's version of the Bill of Rights when it comes to retirement benefits. It tells employers who want to offer protective shells to their employees what they can and cannot do. In simple terms, ERISA looks out for our interests. Together, ERISA and the IRS Code determine the rules for 401(k)s.

In simplest terms, ERISA requires that the plan fiduciaries exercise a considerable level of prudence in the selection and maintenance of the plan investment vehicles. ERISA also imposes the obligation to monitor and perform ongoing review over the investment portfolio of the plan, even though the participants may direct the investment of their own accounts. All of the plan's investment activity should be pursuant to a written investment policy statement.

On October 13, 1992, ERISA section 404(c) (regulations that govern the transfer of investment control to participants) relieved fiduciaries of liability for investment losses *if* the plan permits its participants to exercise control over the investments and if the losses result from the participants' exercise of control.

Hence, most plan sponsors attempt to reduce to the greatest extent possible their potential fiduciary liability under ERISA by transferring the investment allocation responsibility to employees. In other words, don't try suing the company if the stock market drops 1,000 points. It's not the company's fault. Your best insurance policy against investment loss is education.

ERISA does protect your retirement assets from the following:

- **Divorce.** Your current or ex-spouse or your kids could get your 401(k) money, but they would have to take their claim to the judge before that can happen. They would have to ask for a *qualified domestic relations order* (QDRO). A QDRO is a decree, a judgment, or an order from the court that says you must give or set aside a portion of your money for a particular purpose: alimony, child support, settlement of property disputes, etc.
- **Taxes.** The IRS can place a lien on assets, but neither the state nor the city can touch your retirement money.
- **Creditors.** In personal bankruptcy, the one thing you can't lose (at least under current law in 2002) is your 401(k). Your creditors can't force you to withdraw or borrow money from your 401(k) and they can't attach your plan money either. So don't let anyone—including your lawyer—talk you into paying debts with your 401(k). But, beware: IRAs, for the most part, are not afforded the same protection. If you roll your 401(k) plan into a self-directed IRA and then someone sues you, that asset is on the table.

Checks and Balances

It's a good idea to check on your accounts occasionally, even if you're not the suspicious type. Even the best record keepers can make mistakes. Here's what you should look at:

- **Account balance reconciliation.** Confirm that the record keeper has updated your accounts correctly. Pull out your last statement and place it beside your new one. The ending balance on the old statement should equal the beginning balance on the new statement. Add up your contributions for the period of the statement from your paycheck stubs and compare this number with the number the record keeper has posted on your statement.
- **Contribution rate changes.** If you change your contribution rate, make sure you know the effective date. Then check your pay stub to make sure the plan administrator has properly implemented your change.
- **Investment election changes.** If you change your investment allocation, check to make sure the record keeper properly processes your change. Check both the investment of current balances and future contributions, if these are different.
- **Investment returns.** How you track investment returns depends on how frequently your accounts are valued—daily or traditionally.

How can you tell if your company has a good 401(k) plan?

1. Your company offers at least six investment options.
2. You can enroll in your 401(k) after six months or less of service.
3. Your company allows you to direct the investment of company 401(k) matching contributions.
4. Your company pays matching contributions—in cash.
5. You can call or go online to get your account balance or to transact other business.
6. You can roll money from a former employer's 401(k) into your current 401(k).
7. Your company actively works at educating you (provides workshops, newsletters, software, etc.).
8. You have access to independent financial advisors.

You can expect more of your plan's expenses to be paid by you. Make sure that you're getting what you're paying for:

- Is the reporting clear, logical, and understandable? Does it show clearly what your plan owns?

- Do you feel comfortable that your overall communications with the financial consultant are good and that the financial consultant attends to your queries and needs promptly?
- Is your 401(k) plan's performance roughly in line with the performance you expect? Or, is the fund apparently doing much better or much worse than expected? Why is this the case? Is the explanation satisfactory?
- If there are investment restrictions in your guidelines, are these being adhered to?
- Is your manager continuing to apply the style and strategy that you understood would be used in the management of your assets?

Warning Signs

A few indications that your 401(k) account may be in trouble:

1. Your company is having financial difficulties.
2. You can't get any information on the investments in your plan.
3. You have asked for, but never received a summary plan description.
4. Your company has never sent you a statement showing the money that you and/or your employer have contributed to your account. When you finally get a statement, it's for a time period more than six months past due (for example, you get a statement in January for the first or second quarter of the prior year).
5. Most of the 401(k) assets are in a single investment managed or selected by the plan trustees.
6. You notice that the investments have changed in your plan, and you were never told.
7. There's a large drop in your account balance and the stock market is up.
8. Your money has been reallocated to different investments without your instruction.
9. Your account is constantly being affected by adjustments (corrected for errors).
10. Your statement doesn't match up to deductions taken from your paycheck.
11. The major players—plan administrator, trustee, record keeper,

and investment manager—change more than once every two years.

12. You don't recognize the plan's trustees. It's not a financial institution. Be concerned if the trustee *and* custodian are both people within the company.

13. There are large discrepancies between the summary annual report and Form 5500 (annual report filed with the IRS) from one year to the next or the numbers don't seem to pass the "smell test."

What can you do? Start by asking questions. If you get no results, contact the Pension and Welfare Benefits Administration division of the U.S. Department of Labor at 202-219-8211 or **www.dol.gov./dol/pwba**.

Note

1. At the end of 1999, there were 340,000 401(k) plans with 34 million participants. Danny Hakim, "Controlling 401(k) Assets: Fight Brewing over Investment Choices for $1.7 Trillion." *The New York Times*, November 17, 2000.

BECOME AN INFORMED INVESTOR

T A TIME WHEN 401(K) PLAN PARTICIPANTS have greater control over their assets than ever before, it's a sad fact, but few participants are even aware that they can make investment allocations or otherwise direct how their plan contributions are invested. Or, if they are vaguely aware of their rights, they don't know how or where to begin.

Many participants in 401(k) plans have no other investing experience. Few have ever heard of the academic theories of investing. What little information they do have comes from television, newspapers and magazines, or co-worker conversations. Most of this "noise" is misguided, sensationalized, and lacks any theoretical foundation. Many false ideas are so widespread that the public, for the most part, simply accepts them as fact.

Often, the plan contribution election forms are presented to the new employee along with insurance documents, confidentiality agreements, etc. upon hiring—all to be completed and returned the next day. Intimidating legal jargon and overriding priorities of the moment may force a selection of anything familiar, usually whatever low-risk, fixed-income vehicle is available. After all, this is retirement money we're talking about here! But, in truth, that's exactly why you want to take an active role in directing the investments that will become a contributing factor in the comfort level you enjoy later in life.

Even if you need to make a decision immediately, most plans allow the participant the freedom to transfer between investment options on a daily basis. That's not to suggest that you should abuse this freedom by chasing the latest "hot picks" or attempting to time the market. Both are strategies that are costly to implement, have an extremely low probability of success, and are ineffective in adding value. Rather, it's to point out your ability to rebalance, or correct your choices, as you become more informed.

To make informed choices, arm yourself with the basic terminology and strategies in this book and get the specific rules of your 401(k) plan. You may have to ask the Human Resources Department for a copy of the plan's summary plan description. Find out if there is a plan representative or financial consultant available to explain the advantage of various investment alternatives, as well as how the plan is monitored. Most 401(k) plans have a long-term, systematic manner of monitoring any investment progress. If you're going to direct your investments, you will need to know how you can receive periodic performance (gain and loss) results.

Some people think that the money in 401(k) plans is insured against a loss. It depends on what kind of loss you're talking about. Once your money enters the 401(k) trust, any fraud, embezzlement, or other criminal activity that might harm you would be protected by insurance. However, your money is *not* protected against *investment losses*.

Brokerage firms and investment dealers have what is called SIPC insurance, which stands for Securities Investor Protection Corporation and is the equivalent to the FDIC (Federal Deposit Insurance Corporation) that covers your bank deposits. SIPC means that your brokerage account is protected up to $100,000 in cash and another $400,000 in securities. But, most 401(k) money is not held in a brokerage account; it is held in a trust. The Pension Benefit Guaranty Corporation (PBGC) protects defined benefit pension plans only if the plan sponsor has insufficient funds to pay participants, if the plan is terminated, or the company goes under.

The only way to protect against investment losses and still achieve a reasonable growth rate of return is by creating a portfolio with an optimal combination of investments for a specific level of risk. The higher the expected growth of the investments, the higher the risk. The lower the risk, the lower the expected return. Real risk is not the volatility of periodic returns; rather, it is the probability of not having enough money to meet a financial goal, such as retirement.

The only way to protect against investment losses and still achieve a reasonable growth rate of return is by creating a portfolio with an optimal combination of investments for a specific level of risk.

How Aggressive Do You Need to Be?

There are two factors that determine how aggressive you should be. The first is how much of a *gap* there is between the current rate of accumulation of your investments and the financial goals you are trying to achieve. The second is how much *time* you have before retirement; the more time you have to accumulate assets and recover from potential losses, the more aggressive your portfolio can be. Or, you can be more conservative because you will have more time to compound the earnings in lower return investments.

However, if you just woke up to the fact that you have only a few years left and there is a huge gap between your assets and the amount of money you will need, you are going to have to increase your investment risk to get higher returns. This may be opposite from the advice you've been reading in other books. But, aside from greatly increasing the amount you're saving, how else can you make up for lost time?

You can start by identifying all the known variables, such as how much you currently have saved in all your asset pools, the size and frequency of your contributions, the amount of matches, investment allocations, and how much time you have before retirement.

Then, compare your long-term dollar needs with your portfolio performance and evaluate the probability of achieving those goals. In most cases, this evaluation will indicate a shortfall or a gap. At this point, your chances for success in achieving your financial goals are based solely on your current asset allocation and investment strategy. Next, determine the maximum risk exposure you feel comfortable with. This will impact the probability of reaching your target retirement financial goals. If you are too conservative, that probability will decrease. You must make the decision between accepting the downside of volatility and increased risk versus the promise of a higher probability of success. Then, after you have determined the amount of risk you are willing to assume, you must attempt to solve for unknown variables, such as future capital market returns. The focus is on what is reliably predictable. Look at the stock market over different time periods, then adjust your allocation to meet your future risk tolerances. This is where most participants stop, because they don't know how much of an adjustment to make. You may need the help of an advisor or planner.

If you have a long time horizon, you can do things more conservatively because time is on your side. But, if you discover that you still have a large gap, you may have to follow more aggressive strategies, such as concentrating more in equity investments, increasing your contributions, extending the age at which you wish to retire, and investing outside your 401(k) plan. Unfortunately, most people have lifestyle wants and needs that far exceed a reasonable growth rate of return inside their 401(k) plans.

What Is a Reasonable Growth Rate of Return?

An informed investor needs to establish their personal expected *reasonable* growth rate of return. The general rule of thumb is that if you take the percentage of decline tolerance (how much money you could stand to lose) in a given quarter that you are comfortable with, divide that percentage in half, and add a money market rate (typically 3% to 4%). The result is a reasonable rate of growth over a three- to five-year period.

Again, how little or how much risk you take directly affects how much growth you can expect. For instance, if you are willing to take a 10% decline quarterly, divide that number in half (5%), and add 3% to 4%, a reasonable rate of growth that you can expect to capture is 8% to 9% annually over a three- to five-year period.

It is important to know, *and remember,* that there will be some times when you will experience declines in excess of this amount and your returns might be superior at other times.

Figure 5-1 shows what a reasonable expected return is based upon your decline tolerance (column one) over a three- to five-year period. The farther the "riskometer" needle is to the right, the riskier the investment and the higher the potential rewards. For simplification purposes, we are using a five-point scale.

FIGURE 5-1   Investments and risks.

Level of Decline	Target Growth Rate	Approximate Time Frame	Core Strategy	Riskometer
3%	3-5%	0-6 months	CDs, money markets	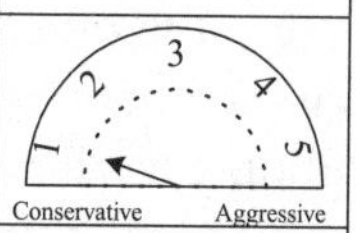
6%	5-6%	3-12 months	Bond fund, money markets, CDs, cash	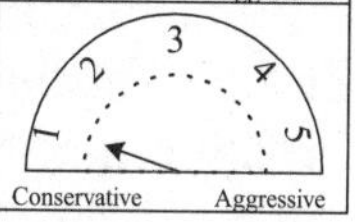
8%	6-8%	6 mos.-2 yrs.	Conservative balanced portfolio, bonds or bond funds–Portfolio 1	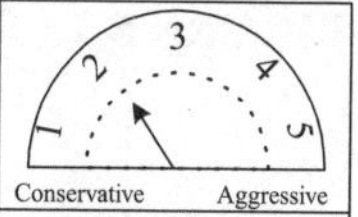
10%	8-9%	18 mos.-3 yrs.	Balanced fund Portfolio 2	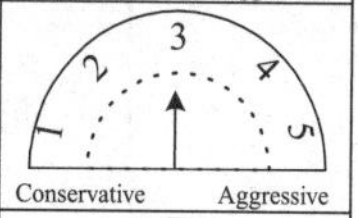
15%	9-11%	3-5 years	Conservative equity fund Portfolio 3	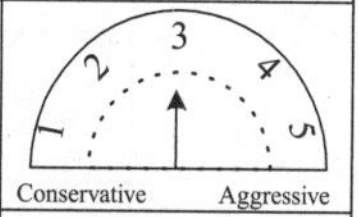
23%	10-13%	5-7 years	Equity fund Portfolio 4	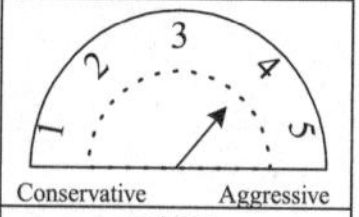
35%	11-14%	5-10 years	Equities Portfolio 4	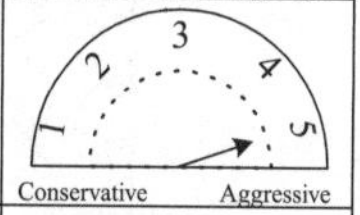
50%	12-15%	5-10 years	Equities Portfolio 4	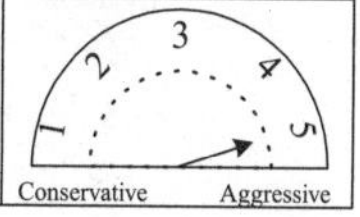

So your next question is probably, how do you measure the risk of an investment?

You may have seen one of the old investment pyramid charts. They're in almost every basic investment book explaining risk and reward: safe investments such as cash at the bottom; bonds, stocks, and real estate in the middle; and more speculative investments at the top. Most 401(k) investors understand this hierarchy, but it's overly simplistic.

In the financial industry, we use what is called *beta* and *volatility*. (*Standard deviation* is another term for volatility.)

Beta is a measure of the risk of an investment compared with that of the market. This is a good way for institutions to measure risk; however, it is often not very useful for individuals since we don't look at risk in relative terms. The market is said to have a beta of 1.0. If a mutual fund has a beta of 0.8, it is said to be 80% as risky as the market.

Volatility is simply investment jargon for frequency and amount of change. Volatility is a measure of *total risk*, instead of *relative* risk like beta. It can be statistically measured using *standard deviation*.

FIGURE 5-2   Risk increases as rewards increase.

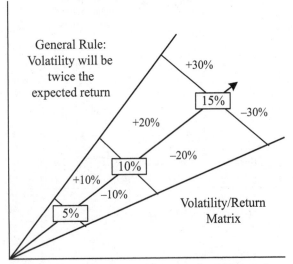

Data by Ibbotson 1926-1994. Investors should never rely solely on this or any chart to make investment decisions.

Standard deviation describes how far from the average performance the monthly performance has been, either higher or lower, and helps explain what the distribution of returns will likely be. The greater the range of returns, the greater the risk (Figure 5-2).

If you invest for a short-term goal, you will probably want lower volatility and be willing to accept lower returns. If you invest for the long-term, you can probably tolerate greater volatility in order to anticipate the potential for greater returns.

People are willing to accept risk when buying real estate because they don't purchase a house thinking that they might sell it tomorrow. They know that, despite occasional drops in the real estate market, their house is probably going to increase in value by the time they've paid off the mortgage in 15 years or longer. The same is true for stocks held over long periods. But for some reason people don't think about stocks the way they think about real estate. "Long term" is next quarter for most people.

When you bought your house, you weren't thinking, "What are housing prices going to do tomorrow?" You were investing over a 10- to 20-year time period, so you bought a home that met your needs and that you believed would increase in worth over the long term. Consider how you would feel about the risk of owning a home if you looked at the market prices every day: "The water main on Sixth Street broke; my house just dropped in value 10%." Odds are you wouldn't be a happy homeowner if you monitored your home's market value daily.

Different investments behave differently during different times. As an example, when the real estate market was booming in the '70s, the stock market had some of its worst years. Large-cap stocks were the top performing asset class in the late '90s, but have done poorly in the last two years. International stocks did poorly the last few years, but so far this year, are one of the best performing asset classes. As you can see from Figure 5-3, in risky investments, it's very hard to predict which will do better at any given time.

> Learn to expect the unexpected. What we want you to do is try to mentally prepare for market "corrections."

Learn to expect the unexpected. What we want you to do is try to mentally prepare for market "corrections," or commonly referred to as a

	1990	1991	1992	1993	1994	1995	1996	1997	1998	1999	2000	2001
Best	Fixed Income 9.0	Small-Cap 46.1	Small-Cap 18.4	Int'l 32.6	Int'l 7.8	Large-Cap Value 38.4	Large-Cap Growth 23.1	Large-Cap Value 35.2	Large-Cap Growth 38.7	Large-Cap Growth 33.2	Fixed Income 11.6	Fixed Income 8.4
	Large-Cap Growth 0.3	Mid-Cap 41.5	Mid-Cap 16.3	Small-Cap 18.9	Large-Cap Growth 2.7	S&P 500 37.5	S&P 500 23.0	S&P 500 33.4	S&P 500 28.6	Int'l 27.3	Mid-Cap 8.2	Small-Cap 2.5
	S&P 500 -3.1	Large-Cap Growth 41.2	Large-Cap Value 13.8	Large-Cap Value 18.1	S&P 500 1.3	Large-Cap Growth 37.2	Large-Cap Value 21.6	Large-Cap Growth 30.5	Int'l 20.0	Small-Cap 21.3	Large-Cap Value 7.0	Large-Cap Value -5.6
	Large-Cap Value -8.1	S&P 500 30.5	S&P 500 7.6	Mid-Cap 14.3	Small-Cap -1.8	Mid-Cap 34.5	Mid-Cap 19.0	Mid-Cap 29.0	Large-Cap Growth 15.6	S&P 500 21.1	Small-Cap -3.0	Mid-Cap -5.6
	Mid-Cap -11.5	Large-Cap Value 24.6	Fixed Income 7.4	S&P 500 10.1	Large-Cap Value -2.0	Small-Cap 28.4	Small-Cap 16.5	Small-Cap 22.4	Mid-Cap 10.1	Mid-Cap 18.2	S&P 500 -9.2	S&P 500 -11.9
	Small-Cap -19.5	Fixed Income 16.0	Large-Cap Growth 5.0	Fixed Income 9.8	Mid-Cap -2.1	Fixed Income 18.5	Int'l 6.1	Fixed Income 9.7	Fixed Income 8.7	Large-Cap Value 7.4	Int'l -14.0	Large-Cap Growth -20.4
Worst	Int'l -23.5	Int'l 12.1	Int'l -12.2	Large-Cap Growth 2.9	Fixed Income -2.9	Int'l 11.2	Fixed Income 3.6	Int'l 1.8	Small-Cap -2.6	Fixed Income -0.8	Large-Cap Growth -22.4	Int'l -21.2

Market leadership changes dramatically from year to year—and predicting the next winning style is impossible. That's why a strategy that includes a variety of investment styles and asset classes makes sense for most portfolios.

FIGURE 5-3   Asset classes perform differently each year.

bear market, when the stock market experiences a decline of more than 20%. At times, the market has gone down and stayed down for a long time. At other times, it just dipped and flipped back up again. The '90s were a time of sharp, quick drops and dramatic movements upward. This might have been because the inflow of information was much faster or it may have been just due to the economy. Our inflation rate was down, our political system was stable, and corporations were generating steady profits. All of these factors combined to create a bull market.

- Since WWII, there have been 42 years with positive market returns and only 11 years with negative returns.
- The best return was +45% in 1954.
- The worst was -29.7% in 1974.
- The median was +16.5%.
- The market has gone down two years in a row only twice, in 1973 and 1974, and again in 2000 and 2001.

The good times in the market have far outpaced the down periods, as you can see. When the economy is healthy and the market is on a roll, stock prices can rise for years. During the last 50 years, the stock market has seen four major bull markets, with moves over 100%; however, there were meaningful declines in between, even in those positive environments.

FIGURE 5-4 Making the right asset allocation decision.

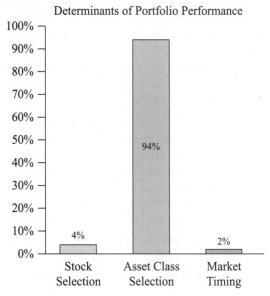

Determinants of Portfolio Performance

The main problems are that you don't have time to be checking on stocks or funds all during the day; and you don't have the expertise to trade in and out of the market during the up and down periods. The point of protecting your plan is also saving your time. Your time is better spent concentrating on your work. As you become an informed investor, you will discover that you can do just as good a job by simply picking the right asset mix and sticking with it.

FIGURE 5-5   Asset mix shift.

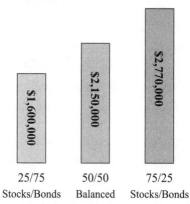

25/75	50/50	75/25
Stocks/Bonds	Balanced	Stocks/Bonds
$1,600,000	$2,150,000	$2,770,000

Jan is 39 years old, $100,000 saved, $90,000 a year income; match 50%; her mix is 75 stocks and 25 bonds. Look at the difference a mix can make. (Assumes 11.35% return for stocks, 5.1% for bonds.)

Understanding the nuts and bolts of 401(k) investing doesn't come naturally, but it's not rocket science either, nor does it require constant hands-on attention. 94% of returns are generated from making the right asset allocation decisions. A portfolio containing only one type of investment is unbalanced, having no dissimilar investments that could help carry the portfolio through tough times. But, a portfolio of six or seven of the same type of mutual funds containing collectively over a thousand stocks is the other extreme.

In the practical application, consider an employee who at age 39 has saved over $100,000 in her 401(k) plan. She's been funneling 8% of her $90,000 yearly salary into her 401(k) plan, plus she receives a 50% percent match from her employer. She is an informed investor, so she shifted her plan to a 75% stock and 25% fixed income mix.

As long as her stocks and bonds maintain their historic norms (11.35% for stocks) and (5% for bonds), she has the potential of retiring at age 65 with over $2,770,000.

Another employee of the same age, saving the same dollar amount with the same employer match, doesn't understand risk and is intimidated by it, so she is investing mostly in fixed income bonds. When she reaches 65, she'll have just under $1.5 million in her account. Not bad, but with a little investment knowledge, she could have had over $1 million more at retirement.

Since we can only guess about the future, we put emphasis on the things you can control—factors such as contribution amounts, retirement age, and investment mix. When you follow a core investment strategy, the subject of Chapter 8, you have to know which mix of asset classes stands the best chance of meeting your objectives. Since risk is mitigated by blending asset classes and expected future returns in an optimal manner, using a core strategy, you never shoot the lights out, but you never go bust either.

Others might claim that this is nothing but a guarantee of mediocrity. Why hold a diversified portfolio of funds where your return will always be in the middle of the pack? But there's nothing mediocre about producing predictable results and being able to sleep at night, while marching steadily toward your financial goals.

Luck Does Play into Investing

Wall Street hates reference to words like "luck"—it sounds too much like a gambling term. We have a somewhat different definition of luck when it comes to investing. Luck is when preparation meets opportunity.

Understanding how markets work is the preparation; continuously investing in the stock market when it has gone up for the last 20 years is the opportunity. Education and preparation

> Wall Street hates reference to words like "luck"—it sounds too much like a gambling term.

increase your probability of good luck. Understand how the economy and markets work together and you will gain insight into what it takes to be successful.

As Dr. Bob Goodman, a noted economist, says, "From an economic standpoint, the environment over the next five years for investors really couldn't be better. We've got everything going for us now. There's an economic turnaround in the works; there's very low inflation, low interest rates, expansionary monetary and fiscal policy, and low energy policy. All the ingredients are there for a long business cycle again, as we had in the '80s and '90s, which means the environment to accumulate wealth could be very good."

Next, broaden your knowledge base by presenting six basic investment concepts that will give you the highest possible probability for success. If you have access to an advisor, work with him or her to develop a personal strategy in the form of a statement of investment objectives; then commit to it in writing and stick with it. You will find a real-world example in the Appendix. Such a statement should articulate clearly what the fund may and may not invest in, the expected long-term goals in terms of performance and volatility, and the general approach to be taken by the manager—whether a private investment manager or a mutual fund manager—for achieving those results.

6

USE THE SIX CONCEPTS OF SUCCESSFUL INVESTING

THE PURPOSE IN UNDERSTANDING THESE BASIC concepts of successful investing is to lessen your fear factor. You will no longer have to play the role of the blind sheep, just following someone else's lead because you're unable to make informed decisions. Simple knowledge is your best protection. You don't have to get a Ph.D. in finance. Once you have a grasp on how these concepts work, you can take an active role in ensuring that these concepts work in your favor, and that you're doing the best you can.

Concept One—Why Diversify?

Diversification quite simply means "not putting all your eggs in one basket," not risking all your money in any one type of investment. That's easy to understand. If something goes wrong with one investment, you won't lose everything.

Since each stock responds differently to changes in the economy and investment marketplace, a short-term decline in one can be balanced by owning others that are stable or going up in value. Mutual funds, by design, hold many different securities and are, therefore, diversified sometimes within one asset class or spread among several different asset classes.

Figure 6-1 illustrates a single investment of $10,000 at an 8% return during 25 years, and compares diversifying the same $10,000 investment into five separate $2,000 amounts, producing various returns.

Three of the five investments in Figure 6-1 showed a lower return than the single investment, but the total for the diversified side was substantially higher. While it's true you would have been further ahead by being invested in just the "hot" stock, selecting that stock is a matter of luck and not likely to be predictable.

> **It's generally not beneficial to invest in a number of assets in the same market segment or in segments that tend to move in tandem.**

However, it's generally not beneficial to invest in a number of assets in the same market segment or in segments that tend to move in tandem. For example, during the '80s, biotech stocks soared; and in the '90s, technology stocks boomed. The risk by investing in only one sector is that all your investments could just as easily decrease in value at the same time. Remember our example in Chapter 3 of the hypothetical island economy from Burton Malkiel's book, *A Random Walk Down Wall Street*.

If you own two investments that move in the same direction at the same time, this would be ineffective diversification. The bottom chart shows how individual risks can be effectively diversified away with investments that do not move in concert with each other. Effective diversification reduces extreme price fluctuations and smoothes out returns (see Figure 6-2).

FIGURE 6-1   Diversification.

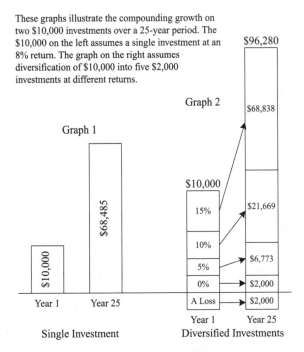

These graphs illustrate the compounding growth on two $10,000 investments over a 25-year period. The $10,000 on the left assumes a single investment at an 8% return. The graph on the right assumes diversification of $10,000 into five $2,000 investments at different returns.

While three of the five investments were a lower return than the single investment, the total for the diversified side was substantially higher.

The key to effective diversification, then, is not the number of assets you are invested in, but the tendency of these holdings to move in low correlation to each other. Technically, correlation is a statistical measure of the degree to which the movement of two variables is related. A *positive* covariance indicates that the returns of two assets rise or fall together, whereas a *negative* covariance means they vary inversely, so that when one holding goes down, others may not drop similarly. A high correlation would mean that two assets move in tandem.

Selecting asset classes with a low correlation to each other is the Nobel Prize-winning secret for achieving more consistent portfolio performance. Academics have actually calculated methods to measure correlation in a portfolio, thereby enabling the volatility or risk of a

FIGURE 6-2 Ineffective diversification and effective diversification.

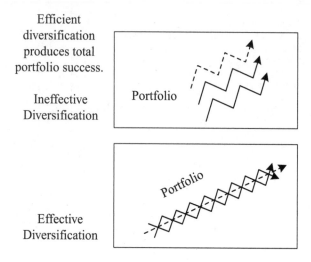

Efficient
diversification
produces total
portfolio success.

Ineffective
Diversification

Effective
Diversification

FIGURE 6-3   Asset classes that have negative covariance.

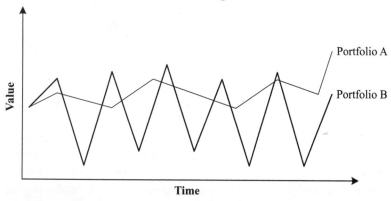

portfolio to be measured. By using these tools, portfolios can be more
systematically created with greater degrees of predictability in terms of
risk and return (see Figure 6-3).

Because of these measurement tools, it is possible to combine in a
portfolio assets that have the potential to generate higher returns due to
their volatile nature, but whose market performances have a low correlation to one another, with the result being that the portfolio as a whole
will actually be less risky than any one of the individual investments,

yet generate a higher overall return than a portfolio made up solely of low-risk investments.

The first step is to diversify *within* each asset class and then also among various asset classes. Now, how do you determine what percentage of each you should own?

Concept Two—The Art of Asset Allocation

Asset allocation is now widely understood by successful investors to be the single most important determinant of the long-term performance of any investment portfolio.

Although the terms "asset allocation" and "diversification" are often used interchangeably, don't confuse the two strategies.

Asset allocation is the way you divide your money among the basic asset classes—stocks, bonds, and cash investments—in order to increase expected *risk-adjusted* returns. The goal is to combine percentages of investments in different asset

> Asset allocation is now widely understood by successful investors to be the single most important determinant of the long-term performance of any investment portfolio.

classes to maximize the growth of your portfolio for each unit of risk that you take. Determining the correct asset allocation can be critical to your investment success.

Asset allocation may be applied to three basic broad categories (stocks, bonds, and cash) or into many narrower segments of each broad category. For example, the stock category can be further segmented into value, growth, small cap, large cap, or foreign. Stocks, as a broad category, have the highest average total return over the long run, but they are often the most volatile in the short run. Cash equivalents have the lowest return, but are the least volatile. Bond volatility falls in the middle. Even if stocks outperform the other asset classes over a period of years, they do not do so every year.

As illustrated in Figure 6-4, over 90% of a portfolio's total return variation is due to the asset allocation of the portfolio. The Brinson, Hood, and Beebower study found that asset allocation accounted for

FIGURE 6-4   Asset allocation chart.

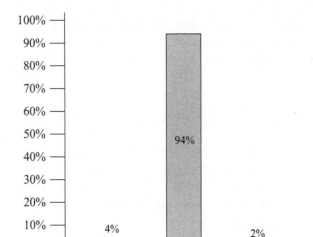

93.6% of the total variation in returns. That means that less than 7% of a portfolio's performance was due to the specific choice of individual stocks and bonds, market timing, security selection, transaction costs, or other miscellaneous influences. Rather, it was the actual allocation that made the difference.

Although it can be a complex topic, you should be familiar with the subtle differences between *strategic* and *tactical* asset allocation.

Strategic asset allocation refers to the most basic allocation decisions of how the assets should be divided among the various broad investment categories. Strategic asset allocation generally entails making decisions that will be implemented over long periods of time.

Tactical asset allocation, on the other hand, refers to the process of active portfolio management that attempts to improve investment performance by shifting the fund's holdings regularly among stocks, bonds, and cash. Tactical asset allocation may at times even reduce diversification, because one asset category is not expected to perform well. Another form of tactical asset allocation would be to choose from multiple investment styles within general asset categories, such as growth or value equity options. Such tactical allocations could be made without the participant disturbing his long-term strategic allocation to equities.

A participant-directed 401(k) plan provides employees with several investment options within different asset classes and requires them to function as their own strategic asset allocators, making general long-term allocation decisions, as well as tactical asset allocators, making month-to-month (or even day-to-day) adjustments to these portfolios.

This creates a serious dilemma for employees, because many may be ill-equipped to make these decisions. Even experienced pension investment executives often lack the expertise or broad perspective necessary to make effective allocation decisions. Professional consulting organizations can assist in determining the proper mix with your specific goals and constraints. But, first, you'll want a simple understanding of the asset classes and investment vehicles that you have to choose among.

Concept Three—Asset Class Investing

Each asset class has specific risk characteristics and specific return characteristics. Let's begin with bonds, often referred to as fixed-income investments, because the income is a percentage set (fixed) by the issuer of the bond. A bond is basically a loan agreement whereby the borrower (bond issuer) agrees to pay to the lender (the investor) a set amount of interest for a set number of years, after which the amount borrowed is paid back to the lender. There are several ways to evaluate bonds, but the most common is by the length of maturity and quality of borrower.

The X axis in Figure 6-5, from the bottom to the top, shows *maturity*—the measure of the time until the bond debt is repaid, whether it is for a long or a short term. Typically, the longer the maturity, the higher the risk and the borrower must pay interest for a longer period of time. The Y axis, from left to right, measures *quality* (from high to low). Typically, the lower the quality, the higher the risk and the higher the yield.

This is because lenders will demand higher interest payments from lower-quality borrowers. In the lower left quadrant would fall short-term, high-quality debt, such as Treasury bills and CDs. In the upper left quadrant are the long-term, high-quality bonds, like government or triple-A-

FIGURE 6-5   Bond investment classes.

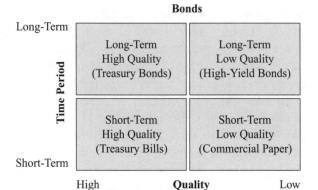

rated bonds. In the upper right quadrant are lower-quality, fixed income bonds; and in the bottom right quadrant are short-term, lower-quality bonds, such as commercial paper. In fact, a bond can be represented anywhere within any of these boxes depending on maturity and quality.

Next are equities, also called stocks, which refer to actually owning an interest or a portion of a company. Investors in stocks are often referred to as "owners." while investors in bonds are often referred to as "lenders." For purposes of Figure 6-6, "cap" refers to the market capitalization of any company, which is determined by the total amount of shares outstanding for the company multiplied by the market price for those shares. Small capitalization companies are generally newer, faster-growing companies which consequently carry higher risk than

FIGURE 6-6   Domestic stocks investment classes.

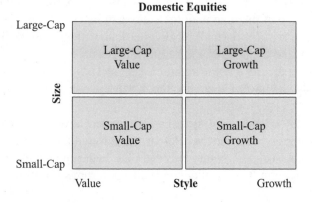

larger capitalization companies which are mature, established well known companies with steadier streams of income and profits.

The figure also refers to value and growth. A "value" company generally has a lower price/earnings ratio, a higher book value vs. market price ratio, and a slower rate of growth than "growth" companies. Growth companies generally exhibit higher rates of growth, higher market prices relative to earnings and book value, and are generally considered riskier and more volatile than "value" companies, but tend to have higher overall returns.

As you can see from the chart, the X axis measures the size of companies from small to large and the Y axis measures companies in terms of value vs. growth. All U.S. companies fit somewhere in this chart depending upon their specific characteristics.

With international equities, instead of measuring the value and growth components, the companies are evaluated as to the markets that they operate in. As can be seen in Figure 6-7, the X axis measures the state of development of the countries, going from an "emerging" market to a fully developed market. The Y axis measures the size of the company. Companies operating in emerging markets are considered riskier than companies operating in developed markets, but also tend to earn greater returns.

One of the key historical facts is that international equities often perform differently than U.S. equities. In many time periods, international stocks will outperform U.S. stocks and in other time periods, U.S.

FIGURE 6-7   International stocks investment classes.

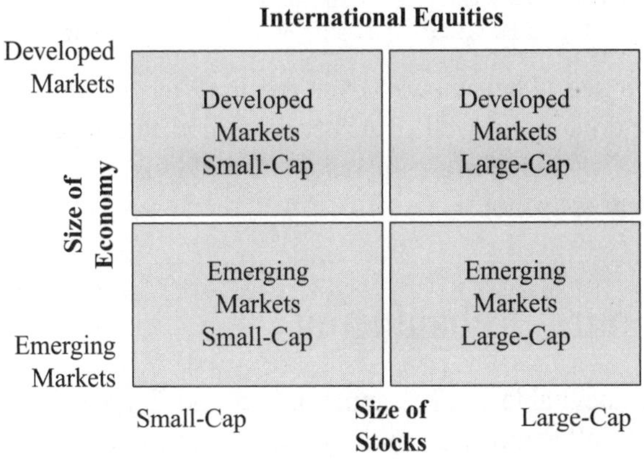

International Equities

	Small-Cap	Large-Cap
Developed Markets	Developed Markets Small-Cap	Developed Markets Large-Cap
Emerging Markets	Emerging Markets Small-Cap	Emerging Markets Large-Cap

Size of Economy (Y axis) — Size of Stocks (X axis)

equities will lead the way. By including both U.S. and international stocks in your portfolio you are reducing risk since the different markets have a low correlation to each other—when one moves up, the other moves in an opposite direction or stays flat.

The best way for an individual to participate in the international markets is through international mutual funds. There are a wide variety of funds, some of which invest based on capitalization ranges of specific country stock markets, while others will invest based on certain international indexes that are run by large investment management firms. Either way, the point is that you are getting diversification and following an asset allocation process by investing internationally.

Figure 6-8 shows the performance over the last 30 years for each of the asset classes.

FIGURE 6-8 Performance of individual asset classes.

	Rate of Return	Beta	Average of Worst 4 Quarters	Average of Worst 4 Years
Large-Cap Growth	12.9	1.13	−29.7	−29.7
Large-Cap Value	15.6	0.83	−17.6	−10.9
Small-Cap Growth	8.9	1.4	−29.5	−28.8
Small-Cap Value	17.6	1.1	−23.2	−18.4
EAFE Index	13.2	0.75	−19.5	−17.8
Long-Term Gov. Bonds	8.9	0.25	−10.3	−5.8
Short-Term Gov. Bonds	7.7	0.0	−0.4	3.8

Source: *First Time Investor's Handbook*, McGraw-Hill, p. 56
EAFE = Europe, Australia, and Far East Index (Morgan Stanley Capital International)

As you can see, when viewed over the long term, these investments have all done quite well. But, keep in mind that in any given one-, three-, or five-year period, the results would look quite different from this 30-year snapshot.

Concept Four—Rebalancing

Given that the inevitable market appreciation and depreciation over time will alter the allocation percentages, participants may need to periodically adjust the balance in their accounts in order to maintain long-term strategic allocations. This is called *rebalancing*.

The idea behind rebalancing is to maintain the same percentages in the various asset classes you have chosen to maintain proper diversification in all market environments. By rebalancing, you may give up some short-term gains if you reduce your holdings of winning stocks prematurely, but you'll also miss the big losses when and if they collapse.

> By rebalancing, you may give up some short-term gains if you reduce your holdings of winning stocks prematurely, but you'll also miss the big losses when and if they collapse.

Many large pension funds rebalanced their equity positions down to their allocation targets as the bull market pushed equity values upward. Then last year, they increased equity positions as the declining markets dropped those positions below targets. As a result, they have been selling high, then buying low. See the logic? When the price is down, you are able to buy more shares. Plus, you're reinvesting the money you've made along with your principal and *compounding* your growth.

Although the mechanics of rebalancing are fairly straightforward, there is an infinite number of methods that could be used to reach that optimal portfolio goal of maximizing returns while minimizing risk. From a theoretical standpoint, two questions arise:

- Is rebalancing effective?
- How often should one rebalance?

What Happens if You Rebalance Using Different Techniques?

Figure 6-9 shows the continuing education report from Provident Investment Council that tested five techniques using 23 years of data (six Russell Indices) to compare their effectiveness and the differences between results from rebalancing annually and results from rebalancing quarterly. Let's look at different rebalancing strategies.

FIGURE 6-9 What happens if you do nothing?

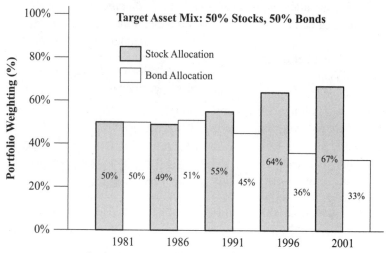

Stocks are represented by the S&P 500 Index
Bonds are represented by the Lehman Brothers Aggregate Index
Data Source: AIM Micropal, Inc.

Let It Ride

This is a passive rebalancing strategy. Under this strategy, the investor simply sits back and allows the style rotation to occur without interference; the market cycles do the rebalancing (Figure 6-9).

Back to the Start

This strategy involves rebalancing all styles back to the original allocation. In the case of diversification across six styles, each would be rebalanced to 16.7% every time rebalancing took place.

Tolerance

This strategy is similar to *Back to the Start,* but it allows a predefined tolerance level around the original allocation percentage. For example, a 2% tolerance level would allow each style to vary between 14.7% and 18.7%. At each rebalancing interval, only those styles that had declined below 14.7% of the overall portfolio or increased to greater than 18.7% would be rebalanced.

Robin Hood

Just as Robin Hood stole from the rich and gave to the poor, this strategy involves taking the gains from the style with the highest weight (highest proportion of the overall portfolio) and giving those gains to the style with the lowest weight at the time of rebalancing. This strategy results in rebalancing only two styles: the one with the highest weight and the one with the lowest weight.

Reverse Robin Hood

This is the strategy unknowingly applied by most individual investors. They usually reduce their holding in the style that has declined the most and increase the style that has recently gained the most. This tactic is known as "chasing the hot dot" (Figure 6-10).

FIGURE 6-10 Comparison of growth from rebalancing annually.

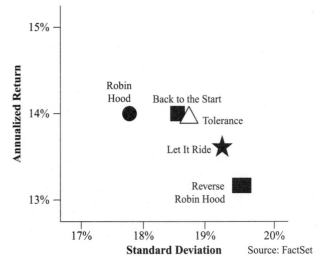

When comparing the risk/return matrix for each of the five strategies based on rebalancing annually, three strategies produced similar results: *Let It Ride, Tolerance,* and *Back to the Start.* But the other two stand out. The *Robin Hood* strategy improved returns and reduced the standard deviation. The *Reverse Robin Hood* strategy detracted from performance and increased volatility (Figure 6-11).

When the frequency of rebalancing was increased to quarterly, the passive *Let It Ride* strategy did not change its results. The two strategies most similar to the passive strategy produced similar results. *Tolerance* and *Back to the Start,* both offered approximately the same return as with annual rebalancing. But the results for the other two strategies

FIGURE 6-11 Comparison of growth from rebalancing quarterly.

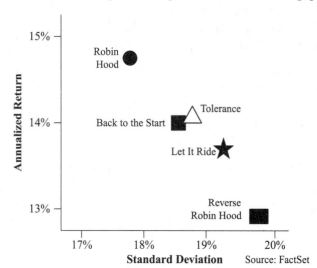

were dramatic. The *Robin Hood* strategy improved the return by almost 1% over the same strategy rebalanced annually and reduced standard deviation by almost 0.5%. The *Reverse Robin Hood decreased* returns and *increased* risk (Figure 6-12).

The study shows that more frequent rebalancing improved results, which would indicate that a style that is outperforming the broad market does not stay in favor for long periods of time. The same holds true for a style that is underperforming the broad market: its out-of-favor status does not sustain for long periods of time.

How to Use These Results to Add Value

Rebalancing an investment portfolio seems simple on the surface, but as you start to think through the method, frequency, tolerance limits, fees, and commissions, the subject becomes quite complex and without easy answers. This is probably not an exercise that an average 401(k) investor would pursue on his or her own. Here's where a qualified advisor can help.

A financial advisor or consultant should be knowledgeable about the various issues surrounding rebalancing and, ideally, should be able to explain them to you in a way that makes the desired method acceptable and practical to apply.

FIGURE 6-12 Growth of $100,000 from different strategies.

$3 million
Robin Hood
$2.5 million
Back to the
Start/Tolerance
$2 million
Let It Ride
Reverse
Robin Hood
$1.5 million
$1 million
$.5 million
$0
1980
1985
1990
1995
2002

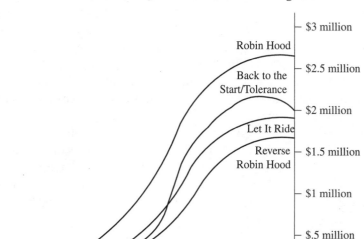

Concept Five—The Power of Compounding

Albert Einstein has referred to the power of compounding as the most powerful force on earth. If you give it enough time, the end result will be many times what the beginning amount was.

Compounding is the process of earning a rate of return on your money that is invested, and then reinvesting those earnings at the same

FIGURE 6-13 The power of compounding.

$221,068
12%
$100,000
10
11.2
12.544
14.0429
15.74
17.63
19.74
22.1068
Year 0
Year 1
Year 2
Year 3
Year 4
Year 5
Year 6
Year 7
Assumes 100% of Portfolio in Stocks

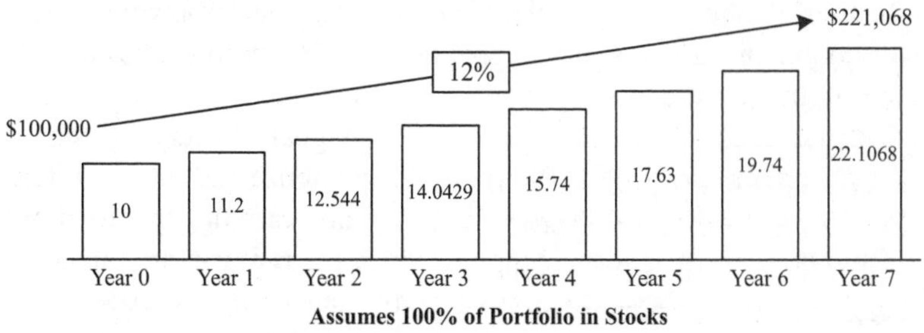

Source: The First Time Investor's Workbook

rate. This can be done with dividends, interest or new contributions. For example, a $100 investment earning compound interest at 10% a year would accumulate to $110 at the end of the first year, and $121 at the end of the second year, and so on. The actual formula is: compound sum = (principal) (1 + interest rate) x (number of years). The essence of the formula is that at the end of each year, interest is earned not only on the original amount but also on all the previously accumulated interest amounts—you are earning interest on interest!

The typical compounding table (Figure 6-14) shows you how a single investment of $10,000 will grow at various rates of return. 5% is what you might get from a Certificate of Deposit (CD) or with a government bond, 10% is about the historical average stock market return, and 20% or more is what you might get if you get lucky and have a hot sector or hot stock working for you.

FIGURE 6-14 How $10,000 grows at different rates of return.

Year	5%	10%	15%	20%
1	$10,000	$10,000	$10,000	$10,000
5	$12,800	$16,100	$20,100	$24,900
10	$16,300	$25,900	$40,500	$61,900
15	$20,800	$41,800	$81,400	$154,100
25	$33,900	$108,300	$329,200	$954,000

A simple way to figure how long it takes your money to double is the rule of 72. Divide the number 72 by the interest rate or rate of return you are earning and the result is the number of years it takes your money to double. For example, if you are earning 10%, your money will double in 7.2 years. If you are earning 12%, it only takes 6 years for your money to double.

> If you can earn just 10% in 20 years, because of compounding, your money will have grown by almost 800%.

A goal of every investor is to maximize the rate of return you are earning, but to minimize the risk you are taking. If you can earn just 10% in 20 years, because of compounding, your money will have grown by almost 800%. That is the Power of Compounding that Albert Einstein was talking about.

Concept Six—The Perspective of Time

Given enough time, investments that might otherwise seem unattractive may become highly desirable. The longer the time period over which investments are held, the closer actual returns in a portfolio will come to the expected average. This means short-term market fluctuations will smooth out.

The real challenge is to commit to a discipline of long-term investing and to avoid compelling investment distractions. Analysis shows that, over and over again, the trade-off between risk and reward is driven by one key factor—*time*. With a long-term view, you can better choose investments that have the best chances for success. By adding the essential ingredient of time to your investment plans, you can almost be assured of success.

Figure 6-15 shows the Nasdaq for two weeks, 3/31/00 through 4/14/00. The Composite was down 27%.

Figure 6-16 represents the Nasdaq for three months. It was down

FIGURE 6-15 Nasdaq Composite 3/31/00-4/14/00.

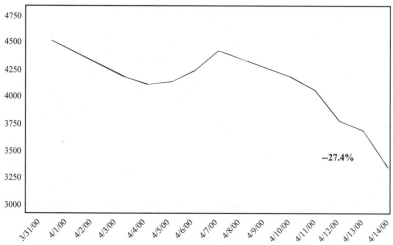

FIGURE 6-16 Nasdaq composite, 3/31/00–6/30/00.

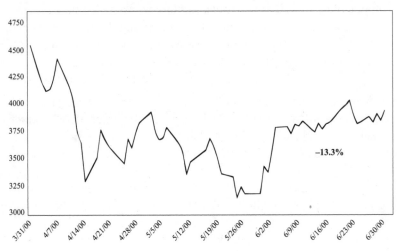

13% over that short period. The real story is in Figure 6-17. Time diminishes risk. When you view the full year, the Nasdaq was up 47%.

No sensible investor would knowingly invest in a stock for only one day, one month, or even one year. Such brief time periods are clearly too short for investment in stocks, because the expected variation in

FIGURE 6-17 Nasdaq composite, 7/1/99–6/30/00.

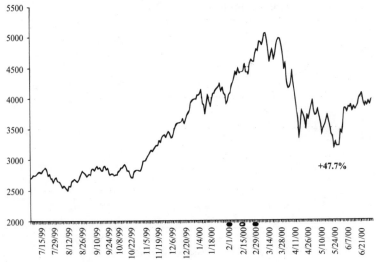

returns is too large in comparison with the average expected return. Such short-term holdings in stocks are not investments; they are *speculations*. Equities become much less volatile the longer they're held. Bonds and money market funds are lower risk, lower return, and can be held a shorter time.

If you study Figure 6-18, you will see that the common stock investments made in any one-year period could have gone up 54% or dropped 43%. But, when you look to any 20-year period, you will see that there are no down years—only gains.

If we measure an investment every three years, rather than every quarter, we can see satisfying progress that wouldn't be apparent on a quarterly measurement. In most cases, the time horizon that investors use as the standard to measure results is far too short, causing dissatisfaction with investment performance. Rather, it is better to give the investment a reasonable period of time to meet your expectations. Often doing less is better.

FIGURE 6-18 Correlation of risk over time.

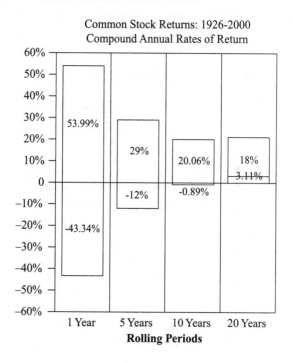

Common Stock Returns: 1926-2000
Compound Annual Rates of Return

How Do You Know if Your Performance Is Good?

Indices are a very important tool for comparing your investments. We use them as a benchmark to ensure that the results of your underlying investments are appropriate and the manager is adding value. For U.S. equities, there are several good indices. An index that measures large-cap value equities is called the Russell 1000 Value Index. If that is hard to find, the Dow Jones Industrial Index is close enough, but not the S&P 500 because it includes growth stocks. For large-cap growth equities, there is the Russell 1000 Growth Index. The Nasdaq composite is also an acceptable measure, but this also includes small cap stocks. If you want to just look at large-cap companies in general, the S&P 500 is a good measure that blends growth and value. If you want to compare small caps, you can look at the Russell 2000 Value Index or the Russell 2000 Growth Index. For international stocks, the Morgan Stanley EAFE (Europe, Australia, and Far East) Index is appropriate. And for bonds, look at the Shearson Lehman Aggregate Bond Index.

Concepts That Are Least Effective

Are there more advanced investment strategies? Yes, but these strategies require more skill and years of experience. You should avoid doing these inside your 401(k) plan.

Individual Stock Picking

Stock picking, in and of itself, is highly risky. Although some plans allow you to buy individual stocks, they may have a limit to the number of times and frequency that you can trade. This could greatly jeopardize your asset. Add to that the huge risk of owning only one stock (the "all your eggs in one basket" scenario) and it becomes an obvious "no-no" for your tax-deferred portfolio.

Many of the rules used successfully in mutual funds do not work in individual stocks. Declines in individual stocks in 2000 were far worse than in any one mutual fund. As in the case of Enron and Global Crossing, declines often don't reverse.

You are as likely to pick a loser as you are to pick a winner. Perhaps you can't resist a "hot tip" or a "getting in on the ground floor" offering or you simply really believe in or want to support a particular company—that's totally OK and it's what makes America great! How can you argue with

> **Many of the rules used successfully in mutual funds do not work in individual stocks.**

someone who bought Microsoft in 1986? Just don't gamble with the strategic portfolio that you built to achieve a certain goal and make sure you don't put all your eggs into that one stock.

Timing the Stock Market

Market timing is the attempt to be in the market when it goes up and out of the market when it goes down. So, market-timers have to be right twice! Successful market timing requires more than clairvoyance; it also demands nerves of steel.

The very best time to buy is when prices have been falling for weeks or months and the market looks absolutely awful. The very best time to sell is the moment when the market is performing superbly. Not surprisingly, few people can bring themselves to do either.

On the contrary, most people much prefer to put money into a stock market that has been booming for a reassuringly long time and they tend to sell investments after the market has been falling. More often than not, they will buy last year's top performer; then last year's top performer will lag and they'll sell it or switch to the next top performer from last year. This results in a "buy high and sell low" (or "lose/lose") environment, with transaction fees adding salt to the wound.

The difficult part of investing is to understand how to keep your greed and your fear in balance. Investing based on how you feel causes you to do significant long-term damage to yourself and your investment program.

Momentum investing, big during the tech stock boom, is another version of market timing. Momentum proponents ride trends to buy stocks with strong upward price momentum. The key again is getting in on time. If you can catch the momentum, then your returns will grow. If you get in too late, then returns can stall. In this strategy, company fundamentals are secondary to analysis of a stock's growth curve.

Informed Investing

All you truly need to do to be a successful information investor is to participate in the free market system and its creation of wealth. Follow the six rules in this chapter, giving yourself enough time, and you'll accumulate more wealth than you dreamed possible.

Obviously, different investment vehicles will provide dramatically different returns. Rather than viewing each specific investment in isolation, it is important to understand the behavior of each in relationship to an overall investment strategy and portfolio.

7

UNDERSTAND YOUR INVESTMENT VEHICLE CHOICES

SINCE MANY 401(K) PLAN PARTICIPANTS FALL INTO the category of "uninformed investors," plan sponsors are faced with the difficult question of "How many and what funds should we offer?" Too many choices may confuse participants; too few may not allow for a successful retirement strategy (see Figure 7-1).

When you receive your enrollment worksheet, you write the percentage of your pay you want to contribute in the space provided at the top of the page. Below that is a list of funds offered. A typical plan offers, on average, six to eight funds covering the available choices—a money market fund, a bond fund, a balanced fund (bonds, preferred stock, and common stock), two or three equity funds, and an international or overseas fund. Your job is to divide your contribution by percentage(s) to your choice(s) of the funds being offered. You can generally pick as few or as many as you want. This will depend on your chosen investment strategy. (See Chapter 8.)

FIGURE 7-1 Typical investment option menu.

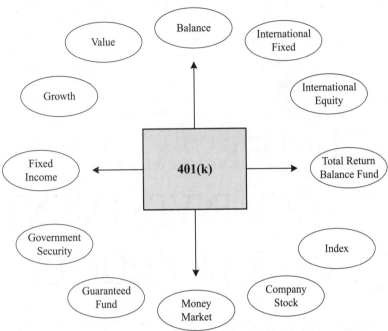

It is also your job to wade through any prospectus included in your enrollment kit. Each mutual fund is required by law to have a prospectus explaining their fund. These are supposed to be in lay terms, but just trying to match the prospectus to the appropriate fund description on the worksheet can be a challenge. Then, to add to the confusion, there is often a supplement to each prospectus. Look for a clue in the words contained in the name of the fund, such as *Growth* or *Balanced,* to match the prospectus with your worksheet investment options.

Following is a description of the vehicles that represent those options.

Mutual funds are the most prevalent of the investment vehicles selected. These funds are directly regulated by the U.S. Securities and Exchange Commission (SEC). The management fees earned by the fund company are calculated according to the average daily net asset value (NAV) and deducted from the account daily. The trend in the mutual fund industry is to have multiple classes for each fund, with one class dedicated to a defined contribution retirement plan. This class, typically Class A, will have lower fees than the retail class. Class B or D shares typically have higher investment fees and/or sales charges that are either charged at the initial purchase or at a subsequent sale.

Think of a mutual fund as a financial intermediary that pools all its investors' funds together and buys stocks, bonds, and/or other assets on behalf of the group as a whole. Each investor receives a certificate of ownership and a regular statement of his or her account indicating the value of their own shares within the total investment pool.

Mutual funds continually issue new shares of the fund for sale to the public. And, every new purchase results in new shares being issued. The number of shares and the price are directly related to the value of the securities the mutual fund holds. A fund's share price can change from day to day, depending on the daily value of its underlying securities. Each share's value is computed by dividing the total value of all the assets held by the fund by the number of shares issued and outstanding.

A stock mutual fund is called an equity fund, which is usually a higher-growth vehicle. Over the last 15 years, the average stock mutual fund has returned about 13.3% on an annual basis. But remember the rule: the greater the return, the greater the risk and volatility. Obviously, an equity mutual fund, because of its investment risk, is not an appropriate investment for your short-term money or for your intermediate money. But, if the time frame for your long-term money is five years or more, an equity mutual fund is a good choice.

> Many of the major fund companies are now coming out with new "retirement shares classes" specifically designated for 401(k) plans.

Many of the major fund companies are now coming out with new "retirement shares classes" specifically designated for 401(k) plans. These funds typically have no front-end fees or back-end sales charges and have only a slightly higher expense ratio, which encourages participants to have access to a broker or advisor who is paid enough to continue to provide services to each participant.

Collective investment funds are similar to mutual funds except they are regulated by the Department of Labor (DOL). Banks and insurance companies generally offer CIFs. The key benefit of collective investment funds is that the fees are variable. Collective investment funds can charge a different fee for each client or charge on a graded basis (generally asset-based). Collective fund fees are generally billed to the plan sponsor as opposed to the participant. These funds are a dying breed, as the trend is toward mutual funds or separately managed funds.

Separately managed accounts are single investment accounts managed by investment advisors for your plan only. No assets are shared with other institutions or retail clients. Separately managed accounts generally have lower fees, but allow the investment advisor or manager of the account to build in performance-based fees. These accounts bill similarly to collective investment funds. A majority of separate account managers have a minimum of dollars they will manage, ranging from several hundred thousand to millions, based on the type of fund and manager.

Lifestyle or asset allocation funds are starting to catch on as a supplement to the traditional mutual funds. Companies generally offer three asset classes: moderate, conservative, and aggressive. Some managers use a fund of funds (multiple mutual funds within each category); others create separate mutual funds with broad mandates that allow them to customize the holdings to meet the three basic objectives. These funds are popular for participants who do not have time to understand the markets or engage in asset allocation exercises, but can fill out a simple questionnaire in order to find out which risk category they should be in. The good questionnaires not only ask about the participant's tolerance for risk, but also focus on the participant's age and net wealth, including house or other income.

Individually directed accounts allow participants to buy and sell in any mutual fund or security available in the retail market. Typically, participants make transactions though a separate 1-800 number directly with a brokerage arm or alliance of the service provider. Many of the service providers allow transactions via the Internet, by phone, or in person. Most do not allow participants to use their own broker. This option has several advantages: 1) participants' account balances are updated on the plan 1-800 line, 2) these balances are generally available for loans, and 3) the account is treated as just another alternative fund option. Most plans charge the participants a fee for this service. The fees typically range from $50 to $300 a year for the account, plus transaction charges ranging up to $30, not including commissions on stock transactions.

Bundled vs. Unbundled Providers

Bundled service providers will tell you that they have an appropriate fund for each investment class. When selecting a bundled service provider, it is clear that investment management fees are used to subsidize defined contribution administrative fees. This is what makes the bundled approach attractive.

Unbundled service providers generally do not provide investment management capabilities, but will advise you not to restrict yourself to just one fund family or to a similar investment style across all funds. What makes the unbundled approach attractive is the ability to offer the best fund in each investment class.

For large plans, separately managed funds may be the best route to take, due to the low investment management fees. For small plans, the service providers (generally record-keeping and consulting firms) offer mutual funds that can subsidize administrative costs, thereby reducing overall costs to the participants.

Each consulting and record-keeping firm generally has a relationship with a mutual fund company or companies. Many consulting firms offer up to 20 different mutual fund families and offer the ability to buy and sell on the same day between mutual fund families.

How Do You Compare?

After reviewing the types of funds and their fee arrangements, the bottom line is long-term fund performance (returns after fees) in the appropriate investment categories. Mutual funds report earnings after fees; collective investment funds and separate account managers generally do not. Our only word of advice is to select funds with a strong long-term record (three to five years) that are consistent performers in the top quartile

> Our only word of advice is to select funds with a strong long-term record.

(or close to it) of their particular asset class.

We're not going to get into analyzing which of the hundreds of mutual funds you should buy. Just look for good, long-term track records, not last year's top performance. Sometimes the worst fund one year may end up to be the best fund the next year, as Figure 7-2 demonstrates.

This chart shows the ranking of the top 20 mutual funds out of 7857 in this particular asset class. Notice that the number-one-ranked fund was number 2898 the following year and the number-two-ranked fund ended up at 7268—almost the bottom. You might wonder, how could they vary so much from year to year? Because no one has a crystal ball.

FIGURE 7-2   Top 20 mutual funds.

1st Year	Next Year	1st Year	Next Year
1	2898	11	7261
2	7268	12	7297
3	45	13	1705
4	7283	14	6
5	262	15	2497
6	6290	16	2719
7	7233	17	7050
8	3473	18	3256
9	7256	19	5383
10	7061	20	7351

How Mutual Funds Work

The manager of the mutual fund uses the pool of capital to buy a variety of individual stocks, bonds, or money market instruments based on the investment objectives as stated in the prospectus. These objectives cover a wide range. Some funds follow aggressive policies, involving greater risk in search of higher returns. Others seek current income and no risk. Since each mutual fund has a specific investment objective, the investor can select a variety of funds to meet asset allocation and diversification needs.

When you purchase mutual fund shares, you own them at *net asset value* (NAV). This is the value of the fund's total investment, minus any debt, divided by the number of outstanding shares. For example, if the fund's investment value is $26,000,000 with no debt and there are 1,000,000 shares outstanding, the net asset value would be $26 per share.

The NAV reflects the daily change in the price of the securities within the fund's portfolio, and is computed at the end of every day that the markets are open for trading. In a regular mutual fund that includes thousands and often millions of shares, the NAV is calculated on a daily basis without commissions, in full and fractional units, with values moving up or down along with the stock and bond markets.

> Despite endless variations, there are basically three broad categories of mutual funds: those aimed at providing immediate income, those oriented toward long-term growth or capital appreciation, or those providing for both.

Many fund management companies offer a number of different types of funds under one roof, often referred to as a *family of funds*. A family of funds might include a growth stock fund, an aggressive growth stock fund, a fund that invests in stocks and bonds, a money market fund, and perhaps many others. Most mutual fund families permit its shareholders to exchange from one fund to another within the group for free, if their personal investment objectives change.

Despite endless variations, there are basically three broad categories of mutual funds: those aimed at providing immediate income, those oriented toward long-term growth or capital appreciation, or those providing for both. The fund's objectives will be stated at the opening of the prospectus, indicating whether the fund emphasizes high or low risk, stability or speculation.

Funds generally fall into one of the following asset class subcategories: stock, balanced, equity income, fixed income, money market fund, tax-free income, and specialized. This is where it can get confusing. The terms most funds use are elementary descriptions of the various types of asset classes. The broad category of "growth" funds generally would include small and large capitalization equity funds. The broad category of "fixed income" would generally include government and corporate bonds, or municipal bond funds. Beyond this, when selecting specific mutual funds, more detailed explanations and categories should be followed.

Active Management vs. Index Funds

In each of these broad asset classes, you can choose an *index* fund. An index fund is typically low cost because the manager only passively invests in whatever stocks are contained in the specific index. The fund performance will generally be the same as the related index. In contrast, an "actively" managed fund is where the investment manager actively engages in the buying and selling of securities based on their relative merits of risk and reward. In essence, the manager is actually managing the fund and not "passively" following an index.

Types of Mutual Funds

Equity Funds

Stock funds emphasize growth. Dividend payouts will typically be low. These funds stress capital appreciation rather than immediate income.

Bond Funds

The key advantage of a bond fund, in contrast with individual bond issues, is that the funds pay income at least monthly with reinvestment possible at the current yield of the fund. A bond fund is always replacing bonds in its portfolio, thereby, actively managing the average maturity of the bonds. In this way, the manager is able to control the risk and reward of the portfolio, as well as the amount of income the portfolio generates. The two main risks associated with a bond fund is market risk if interest rates rise, and credit risk if the quality of the borrowers declines.

Growth

A growth mutual fund is typically defined as one that invests in companies that are exceeding the growth of the economy. Investors look for companies and industries with a strong growth trend in sales and earnings. Growth companies typically sell at high price/earnings (P/E) ratios, reflecting the expectation that their growth will continue and that the earnings will eventually "catch up" with the high valuations awarded the companies. Growth companies and growth mutual funds can cover all capitalization ranges.

Large-Cap Growth. An investment strategy that invests in stocks of large high growth companies with an average capitalization of approximately $7 billion or greater.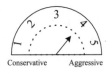

Mid-Cap Growth. An investment strategy that invests in stocks of mid-sized companies with an average capitalization of between $2 billion and $7 billion.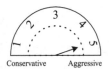

Small-Cap Growth. An investment strategy that invests in stocks of smaller companies with an average capitalization of less than $2 billion.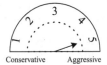

Value

Value stocks often have low book-to-market ratios, which means the stock is trading at a low price compared with its book value. (Book value is defined as the company's assets on a balance sheet, less its liabilities, and is often figured on a per/share basis.) In addition, the price/earnings ratio is generally lower for value stocks, and as such, is generally considered to be less volatile and less risky. As with growth stocks, value stocks can cover all capitalization ranges.

If a company has a book value of $15 per share and the stock trades at $12, it may be perceived as a bargain.

Large-Cap Value. An investment strategy that invests in stocks of large companies with an average capitalization of approximately $7 billion or greater.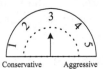

Mid-Cap Value. An investment strategy that invests in stocks of mid-sized companies with an average capitalization of between $2 billion and $7 billion.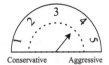

Small-Cap Value. An investment strategy that invests in stocks of smaller companies with an average capitalization of less than $2 billion.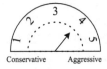

Value and growth stocks tend to behave differently. There are market cycles when value stocks outperform growth stocks, and other periods when growth stocks outperform value stocks. In general, a growth investor's returns are more volatile than a value investor's returns. Both styles in a portfolio can even out performance over time. When one group is underperforming the market, the other is outperforming it. At the end of long periods of time, the annualized rates of return for both growth and value stocks tend to be close to each other.

International Equities

Read the prospectus to determine whether or not the fund tries to protect against fluctuations in the value of the dollar. These moves can have a significant effect, both positive and negative, on funds that do not hedge against currency fluctuations. The types of international funds include the following.

Diversified International Blend Funds. Typically leave control in the hands of the manager and they shift investments across countries and underlying stocks between growth and value.

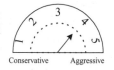

Diversified Emerging Market. Focus their investment on those economies that are still developing and growing. These represent some of the most volatile funds.

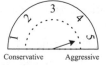

International Growth. The focus of their portfolio is on stocks of high-growth international companies.

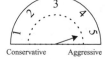

International Value. The focus of their portfolio is on stocks of undervalued companies worldwide.

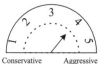

Balanced Funds

A balanced mutual fund includes two or more asset classes other than cash, typically, equities and fixed-income securities in varying percentages. These portfolios stress three main goals: income, capital appreciation, and preservation of capital.

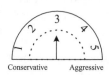

This type of fund balances holdings such as bonds, convertible securities, and preferred stock, as well as common stock. The mix varies depending on the manager's view of the economy and market conditions.

Fixed-Income Funds

Conservative   Aggressive

The advertised investment objectives of fixed-income funds are safety and income, rather than capital appreciation, but we're skeptical. Income funds invest in bonds of all types, including corporate and government bonds, government-insured mortgages, and municipals. Some bond funds may own stocks in small percentages, but these are usually preferred shares or convertible bonds that may trade like common stocks. These "hybrid" fixed-income funds carry a 2% higher degree of risk, but do offer the potential of some capital appreciation.

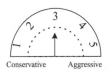

Conservative   Aggressive

U.S. Fixed Income. These are funds that invest in all types of U.S. bonds, including government and corporate bonds. They will typically invest in higher-quality investments with little risk of default across a broad range of maturities.

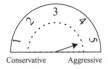

Conservative   Aggressive

High Yield. These funds typically invest in low-quality debt and are subject to a high risk of default. They, therefore, tend to offer a higher yield. They also tend to trade and be priced more like common stocks.

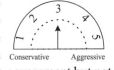

Conservative   Aggressive

Government. These funds invest in debt from the U.S. government. They are by their nature quite conservative, depending upon the maturity of the underlying bonds. They generally invest in all types of government bonds, including those backed by the government but not directly issued by the government.

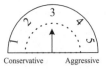

Conservative   Aggressive

International Fixed Income. These funds specialize in investing in bonds of foreign governments and are usually riskier than U.S. investments since they also are impacted by fluctuations in the foreign currency markets.

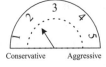

Conservative   Aggressive

Global-Bond Funds. These funds invest in foreign and U.S. bonds. Historically, global bond funds have outperformed domestic bond funds, but you do assume the additional risk of foreign currency fluctuation.

Money Market Funds

Money market funds are the safest type of mutual
funds if you are worried about the risk of losing
your principal. Money market funds are like bank
savings accounts in that the value of your invest-
ment does not fluctuate. Money market funds, however, are not insured
like bank certificates of deposit.

Conservative   Aggressive

Understanding the Prospectus

A survey by the Investment Company Institute, the mutual fund industry's trade group, discovered that only half of the fund shareholders consult a prospectus before investing. With more than the estimated ten thousand mutual funds to choose from, many investors feel overwhelmed
when comparing possible investments, particularly when they have to
wade through prospectuses that are often complicated and confusing.

The good news is that the SEC is recommending new rules, including requiring the translation of the fund booklets into easily understood
language and the creation of a clearly written one-page summary—a
streamlined profile that includes a mutual fund's vital statistics. Such
documents must be updated at least once a year.

Investment Objective. At the core of the prospectus is a description of
the fund's investments and the portfolio manager's philosophy. The
objective should outline what types of securities the fund buys and the
policies regarding the quality of those investments. For example, if the
fund has more than 25% of its assets in one industry or holds bonds
with ratings that would qualify them as high yield (junk), these policies
must be included in the prospectus. Essentially, all policies of the
investment manager, as well as the objectives of the investment, must
be stated clearly in this description.

Performance. The SEC has mandated that all fund performance be
reported uniformly in every prospectus, thereby, allowing a fair and
accurate comparison between funds. Annualized performance over 1, 5
and 10-year time periods must be reported, along with exposure information, as well as tax information. Also shown is the portfolio turnover

rate which reveals how actively the fund trades securities. The higher the turnover, the greater the fund's brokerage costs.

Risk. The prospectus also must clearly describe the risks inherent in the fund, as well as the potential rules in any of the securities that the fund might invest in. For instance, a fund that invests in only one portion of the economy may offer greater risk than a highly diversified fund, while a fund that invests in well-established companies may be less risky than one that favors start-up companies.

There are other risks associated with certain types of funds or securities. Bond funds are susceptible to interest rate changes, while fixed-income savings and investment vehicles are subject to inflation risks. All of these must be described in the prospectus.

Fees. Funds are required to summarize their fees in a table in the front of the prospectus. Other charges to consider are minimum fees for subsequent investments or fees for switching from one fund to another in the same family. Management and accounting fees and the cost of printing and mailing reports to shareholders are internal charges that should also be evaluated. Generally, a company that keeps its expenses—excluding sales fees—at 1% or less of its assets is considered a low-cost fund. A fund whose expenses are above 1.5% of its assets is viewed as high-cost. Fees earned by the portfolio manager or investment advisor are also clearly spelled out under "investment advisory" fees.

Management. When you're investing your money into a mutual fund, you're paying for professional management. Actively managed funds charge more than passively managed index funds. Likewise, management fees as a percent of the total assets are generally lower for larger funds than in smaller funds. Find out whether the portfolio is managed by an individual or committee.

Services. This section will tell you if features such as check-writing or automatic investing are available.

Buying or Selling Shares. This information details how to get in and out of a fund and whether there's a charge for purchasing or redeeming shares. This section also described the different classes of shares and the costs and expenses associated with each class.

Statement of Additional Information. Also called Part B of the prospectus. Funds must provide this information free on request.

Other Things You Should Know

Management Fees. Because of the large amounts of assets under management, investment companies are able to offer *economies of scale*, or competitive fee schedules, to their customers. Fund costs are an equally important factor in the return that you earn from a mutual fund. Fees are deducted from your investment. All other things being equal, high fees and other charges depress your returns.

The management fees charged depend on the complexity of the asset management demands. Foreign equity management requires substantially more research, specialized implementation, and higher transaction costs than the management of a U.S. government bond fund. Asset management fees reflect those differences. Equity mutual fund fees are higher than bond mutual fund fees. Actively managed funds typically have higher fees than index funds, since they seek to outperform the indexes and must, therefore, invest substantially in research and are typically more active in trading.

Remember to compare the proverbial apples with apples—in this case, similar equities to equity mutual funds and similar bonds to bond mutual funds.

Caution: Don't concentrate on fees as much as you concentrate on after-fee performance. While everyone talks about fees, it's far more important that managers earn their fees than that they charge very little. This is obviously not so for index funds, where cost should be the only difference among the funds.

Sales Charges. Sales charges (or loads) are commissions paid on the purchase of mutual funds and are subtracted either from the initial investment amount (purchase) or redemption proceeds (sale) received upon sale depending on the class of shares purchased. In the past, all commissions were simply charged up front, but that has changed. There are now several ways that mutual fund companies charge fees.

A *front-end* load mutual fund charges a fee when an investor buys

FIGURE 7-3 Fee comparisons of various mutual funds.

Mutual Fund	Annual Performance	Management Fees	Net Performance
Foreign Equities	12.5%	1.25%	11.25%
U.S. Large-Cap	12.5%	1.00%	11.5%
U.S. Small-Cap	13.0%	1.20%	11.8%
Investment-Grade Bonds	7.8%	0.65%	7.15%
High-Yield Bonds	9.25%	0.75%	8.5%
Foreign Bonds	9.25%	0.90%	8.35%

it. These shares are generally referred to as "A" shares. Loaded mutual funds can also be *back-end* load—having a deferred sales charge—and are sometimes known as *B shares*. This class of shares generally has higher internal costs. If you decide to redeem your shares early, usually within the first five years, you pay a surrender charge (back-end load).

A customer who redeems shares in the first year of ownership would typically pay a 5% sales charge. The amount would drop by an equal amount each year. After six years, the shares could be redeemed without further charge.

With *A shares*, you pay the commission all at once, upon initial purchase.

B shares have a contingent deferred sales charge that is charged upon the sale of the fund within the first five or six years. These carry higher internal expenses.

C shares typically have even higher internal expenses than A shares, but only impose a 1% sales charge if the shares are sold within the first year. After that, there is no sales charge, but the higher internal expenses continue.

No-load mutual funds do *not* mean *no cost*. Some no-load funds charge a redemption fee of 1% to 2% of the net asset value of the shares to cover expenses, mainly incurred by advertising. No-load funds also have ongoing internal expenses just like load funds.

Expense Ratio. A fund's expense ratio is the total percent of assets deducted from the fund each year. (The fees are deducted in very small amounts on a daily basis.) Expense ratios vary greatly from fund to fund. Vanguard, well known as one of the fund industry's frugal funds, carries a median expense ratio of just 0.25%. Many investors consider the expense ratio to be the most important aspect of a mutual fund. Returns aren't guaranteed; expenses are.

> Many investors consider the expense ratio to be the most important aspect of a mutual fund. Returns aren't guaranteed; expenses are.

For example, take a hypothetical fund with an expense ratio of 1.3% and one with an expense ratio of just 0.2%. If you invest $25,000 in each and they both average a 10% return compounded over 20 years, the fund with the lower fee results in a not-so-insignificant $31,701 additional in your account.

Diversification in the Fund. A mutual fund is typically invested in anywhere from 25 up to 500 or more securities, depending upon the investment manager's philosophy and the size of the fund. Proper diversification ensures that the fund earns the highest possible return at the lowest possible risk given the objectives of the fund. As such, not all mutual funds are considered to be diversified portfolios.

Dividends. Dividends and capital gains (the profits from a sale of stock) generated inside the mutual fund are paid annually in proportion to the number of mutual fund shares you own. So even if you invest only a few hundred dollars, you get the same investment return per dollar as those who invest millions.

Automatic Reinvestment. One of the major benefits of mutual funds is that both dividends and capital gains can be reinvested automatically and converted into more shares (compounding effect).

Liquidity. One of the key advantages of mutual funds stems from the liquidity. You can sell your shares at any time for the closing price on the day of sale as computed at 4 PM EST. In essence, mutual funds have a "ready market" for their shares every day the market is open.

Switching, or an exchange privilege, is offered by most mutual funds through *family* or *umbrella* plans. Switching from one mutual fund to another accommodates changes in investment objectives as well as changes in the market and the economy. *Outside* of a retirement plan, switching between mutual funds creates tax implications. For instance, if you redeem a growth fund and buy a municipal bond fund, you may have to pay taxes on the gains you earned while owning the growth fund.

Full-Time Professionals. When you invest in a mutual fund, you are hiring a team of professional investment managers to make complex investment judgments and handle complicated trading, record-keeping, and safekeeping responsibilities for you. Their job is to sift through the thousands of available investments in order to choose those that, in their judgment, are best suited to achieving the asset class investment goals of a fund as spelled out in the fund's prospectus.

Statements. Any mutual fund in which you participate will send you a year-end statement itemizing the income, as well as capital gains, you've received. You should save this sheet, along with other records of dividends, tax-exempt interest, capital gains distributions, and additional investments made as well as records of the amounts received from the sale of shares for future tax purposes.

Audited Performance. All mutual funds are required to disclose historical data about the fund through their prospectus—returns earned, operating expenses and other fees, and the rate of trading turnover. All mutual funds are registered investments, which means the SEC audits these disclosures.

Independent Custody. Mandated by the Investment Company Act of 1940, independent custody means that it's very difficult for a fund manager to use the money for his or her own purposes. The money manager of a mutual fund has no direct access to investors' cash. The custodian who controls the underlying securities allows them to be traded or exchanged with other institutional investors only after getting proper documentation from the manager.

> Mandated by the Investment Company Act of 1940, independent custody means that it's very difficult for a fund manager to use the money for his or her own purposes.

The fund manager checks a daily account balance sheet and "new monies" are invested according to the mutual fund's investment policy.

Independent custody means a mutual fund's parent company can go belly up without any loss to the fund's shareholders, because their assets are held apart from other funds. Contrast this business structure with the far less restrictive setup between individual investors and a real estate promoter, for instance, or investors and a stockbroker who may have direct access to clients' accounts. In any number of notorious incidents, individuals in such a position have taken the money and run.

The limited partnerships of the 1970s and 1980s were an excellent example of a poor business structure. During those years, many unregulated and unregistered limited partnerships were formed and investors sent their money directly to the limited partnership company. An unscrupulous promoter could simply write himself or herself a check. Financial scandals were pervasive.

How to Read Newspaper Mutual Fund Tables

Figure 7-4 provides an explanation of how to read and understanding the information on mutual funds found in newspapers. This figure shows all the possible information that might be included. Many newspapers do not list all the categories shown here.

In nearly any listing you'll find the following information about the fund:

- The abbreviated fund's name. Several funds listed under the same heading indicate a family of funds.
- A columne headed "Sell," is the net asset value (NAV) price per share. As you'll recall, the NAV is the amount per share you would receive if you sold your shares (less deferred sales charges, if any). So, on any given day, you can determine the value of your holdings by multiplying the NAV by the number of shares you own.
- Another column, headed "Buy," is the *offering* price (sometimes called the *asking* price). This is the price you would pay if you purchased shares that day. The buy price is the NAV plus any sales charges. If the fund is a no-load, "NL" will appear in this column (meaning there is no upfront sales charge.

FIGURE 7-4 How to read newspaper mutual fund tables.

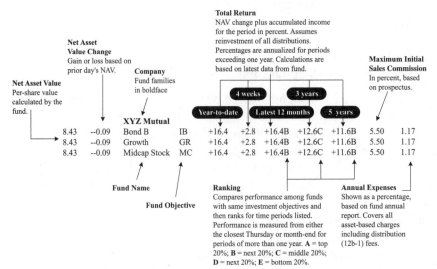

- Another column shows the change in NAV from the day before, either up or down.

Depending on the publication, you may find additional informati-no about the fund's performance, and even 800 numbers to get the fund's prospectus.

The Rating Game

The mutual fund rating game works much the same arbitrary way as the old dating game on television. Investors use ratings of mutual funds that are listed in newspapers and magazines as a guide to help them pick funds that are the right ones for the portfolio. Other tools to eval-uate mutual funds include news accounts and the funds' annual reports. Plus, you can find the following resources online or at most libraries.

Lipper Analytical Services
Mutual fund research company
Phone: 212 393-1300
Fax: 212 393-9098
Web site: **www.lipperweb.com**

Morningstar

Mutual fund research company; covers mutual funds, closed-end funds, and even stocks

Phone: 312 696-6000

Fax: 312 696-6001

Web site: **www.morningstar.com**

Choosing an A-rated fund would be a logical, quick, and easy way to choose a fund, but are these ratings actually useful? Rating services measure funds during different time periods and use different criteria, which could affect a fund's ranking.

Let's consider mutual fund ratings in *The Wall Street Journal* as compiled by Lipper Analytical Services. Lipper awards an A to funds that have returns in the top 20% of their category. The next 20% get B's and so on, through C, D, and E.

This means that the Vanguard Index 500 Fund is ranked in the top 20% of all similar funds and the Vanguard Index Small Company Fund only ranks in the middle of its peer group. Likewise, for the last three years, the Vanguard Index European Fund has managed the highest rating of A, while the Vanguard Index Pacific Fund gets only a D for the previous 12 months.

Index funds are the easiest of all funds to rank; they simply mirror broad market segments and disclose exactly what's in their portfolios. Actively managed funds are much harder to classify than index funds, because they have changing styles, fluctuating asset allocation, and other complications. If Lipper can't classify index funds correctly, how accurate can other ratings be?

And, did you know that many mutual fund managers increase the risk level of their portfolios and try to enlarge their returns over short periods of time right in the middle of the year to improve their funds' rank? Good ratings bring money into mutual funds, bonuses to managers, and so on. Naturally, managers will do whatever they need to do to improve their ratings.

> Did you know that many mutual fund managers increase the risk level of their portfolios and try to enlarge their returns over short periods of time right in the middle of the year to improve their funds' rank?

Make sure you are comparing *apples with apples*. Side-by-side comparisons of funds should soon be available. Information will be more visible in a shorter document available online. Disclosure will include a 10-year bar chart, a fund performance, a table comparing performance with market index, and a description of the risk involved in the investment. A three- to six-page profile also will summarize the fund's fees, risks, and investment objectives.

Investors who are truly devoted to learning about financial matters and who follow financial news, reading enough to keep themselves well informed, may be able to do this for themselves—but there is nothing embarrassing about seeking professional guidance for your investments.

Just as important as selecting the right investments is building an appropriate core investment *strategy* that the investor can adhere to that delivers a consistent and specific result.

C H A P T E R

BUILD A CORE
INVESTMENT
PORTFOLIO

WE HAVE TALKED ABOUT THE VALUE of the 401(k) plan as a wealth accumulation tool, where to get the money to invest, and the importance of becoming informed enough to protect yourself, and we have given you a basic understanding of six successful investing strategies. Now, how do you put all that together to create your investment portfolio without it becoming your full-time job?

Managing an investment portfolio involves accumulating and analyzing many specifics, such as a forecast for return for each of the investments, calculating how they work together in terms of generating risk in that portfolio, selecting and monitoring fund managers, reviewing your progress, and rebalancing. It comes as no surprise that most participants just want to check a box on the form and forget about it until they leave that employer.

> This chapter will show you how to select a portfolio that will support a core investment strategy and narrow all your future 401(k) investment decisions.

What if we can show you how a minimum amount of effort can make a substantial difference in your future financial well-being? Creating a core investment strategy will position your investments out ahead of where the market will go next. This chapter will show you how to select a portfolio that will support a core investment strategy and narrow all your future 401(k) investment decisions.

The first step is to determine your core allocation or mix of stocks and bonds. This is the fundamental decision that will determine the degree of overall risk in your portfolio, since bonds are used to reduce risk, while stocks are used to create capital. If you have a higher percentage of bonds, then your portfolio will be less volatile, with less overall risk. Of course, the total portfolio over time will also earn less than if the portfolio were invested solely in stocks, but this is the trade-off between risk and return.

Historically, going back 75 years, high-quality stocks as represented by the S&P 500 have returned on average about 10.5% per year, while bonds over the same time frame have returned approximately 5% per year. During this same time frame, stocks were three times as volatile as bonds, and therefore three times as risky. The amount of risk, or volatility that you want to assume will determine your core allocation between stocks and bonds.

Once you have determined the percentage of your assets that is going to be invested in stocks, the next decision that must be made is to determine what percentage of "growth" stocks and what percentage of "value" stocks you will be comfortable with. As a general rule, growth stocks are more volatile than value stocks, even though over long periods of time, the total returns of each category of stocks has been somewhat similar.

Growth managers seek high-growth companies that are generally more expensive. Value managers seek their returns by buying low-priced stocks that are currently overlooked or out of favor but are expected to come back into fashion. If you've ever booked discount airfares during off-peak travel times, you've practiced what value managers preach.

On the surface, buying out-of-favor stocks may appear to be a risky proposition. But, when you look deeper, you'll see that value stocks feature two characteristics that help reduce their volatility:

- Below-average prices. Because value stock prices are already cheap, their downside potential is somewhat limited when the markets go down.
- Above-average dividends. Value stocks normally pay higher dividends, which help to cushion the impact of negative returns.

Growth mutual fund managers, on the other hand, prefer the stocks of already fashionable, fast growing companies and are willing to pay a premium for such accelerated growth. Put another way, value aims to buy low and sell high, while growth is content to buy high if it means selling even higher.

Both value and growth styles have their merit which is why the "core" equity portion of your portfolio should have a blend of both value and growth.

Value and growth investments rarely perform in lockstep. In some years, growth performs better. In other years, value comes out on top. By blending these two very different styles, you balance your risk and enhance your opportunities for reward, as shown in Figure 8-1.

The chart shown in Figure 8-2 tracks three portfolios for 10 years. Notice the significant difference between the returns of the all-growth and all-value portfolios in 1999. Except for the period of 1994-1997, one style strongly outperformed the other. But when you look at the 10-year cumulative returns, all three portfolios resulted in 17%-plus returns. Maybe the middle portfolio smoothed out the year-to-year volatility somewhat, but the bottom line is they're all pretty close.

You will notice that these results are quite high, since we have gone through an amazing market where both bonds and stocks have done extremely well. As mentioned earlier, the long-term average return of the stock market is closer to 10-11%.

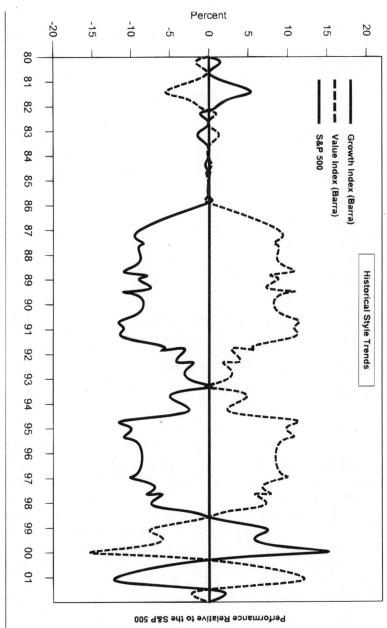

FIGURE 8-1 Core blends value and growth chart.

FIGURE 8-2 A history of three portfolios.

Year	Growth 100%	50-50 Blend	Value 100%
1991	41.16	32.76	24.61
1992	5.00	9.41	13.81
1993	2.90	10.51	18.12
1994	2.66	0.35	−1.99
1995	37.19	37.77	38.35
1996	23.12	22.43	21.64
1997	30.49	32.86	35.18
1998	38.71	26.81	15.63
1999	33.16	20.25	7.36
2000	−22.42	−7.69	7.02
10 Years (Annualized)	17.33	17.68	17.38

Source: Frank Russell Company. Growth and value returns are those of
the Russell 1000 Growth and Russell 1000 Value indices. Past
performance is no guarantee of future results.

Building the Portfolio

To help you get started, we have constructed four model core portfolios,
ranging from conservative to aggressive, to serve as guideposts, using
only very basic allocations of equity mutual funds, bond funds, and
cash. (A professional advisor might certainly do something more
sophisticated.)

We blend a large-cap growth fund and a large-cap value fund to
create effective diversification; we do the same for small cap and add
in an international component for additional diversification.

These models are typical for a wide range of investors with different degrees of risk tolerance (Figure 8-3).

Since the "core" portion of your portfolio represents the fundamental
base of your overall portfolio, you need to decide how much of your

FIGURE 8-3. Four core model portfolios.

	Large Stocks	Small Stocks	Int'l Stocks	Bonds
Core Portfolio 1: Conservative	20%	10%	10%	60%
Core Portfolio 2: Balanced	30%	15%	15%	40%
Core Portfolio 3: Growth	40%	20%	20%	20%
Core Portfolio 4: Aggressive	50%	25%	25%	0%

investments will be represented by the "core" holdings. These core holdings all include the bond portion of your allocation. The portfolios are rebalanced annually based on the weight assigned to each asset class. The best and worst annual returns for each portfolio are calculated by compounding twelve best or worst months during a calendar year. The average annual return is an arithmetic average during the designated time period. The asset class weightings of each portfolio are listed in Figure 8-3.

Since 401(k) plans are not taxed during accumulation, the following performance is based on a buy-and-hold since 1970 and do not include the impact of taxes or expenses of any kind. Typically, if you buy index funds, you will reduce these numbers by about 50 basis points.

The final decisions that need to be made, then, are: What specific asset classes should be included in each of the "core" allocations? How much should be in large capitalization value or large capitalization growth? How much should be allocated to international equities? What percentage should be allocated to small capitalization value stocks or small growth stocks? And, finally, of the fixed income investments, how much should be allocated to government bonds and how much should be allocated to corporate bonds? An example of these various asset classes is shown in the chart below.

The reason we chose to average the worst four quarters is because it takes out some of the really horrendous periods that occurred and blends them down. The same with the average of the worst four years; this way you get a realistic expectation of what a really bad year could look like. So you could absolutely expect to experience a decline of this magnitude and not be too surprised. Of course, it could be a little worse, or not as bad (Figure 8-4 or shown graphically in Figure 8-5).

FIGURE 8-4 Performance of model portfolios.

	Aggressive	Growth	Balanced	Conservative
Rate of Return	14.2	13.2	12.2	11
Beta	.99	.82	.65	.48
Average Worst 4 Quarters	−15.6	−12.22	−8.9	−6
Average Worst 4 Years	−20	−16.3	−12	−8.3

The following rates of return for each of the core portfolios (Figures 8-6, 8-7, 8-8, and 8-9, with the conservative portfolio first) were computed using actual past history of the various asset classes, and then averaging the rates of return over long periods of time. The portfolios were also rebalanced annually based on the relative percentages assigned to each asset class. Finally, the best and worst months in any calendar year were averaged together to determine what the maximum quarterly downside was for each of the models. And, the best and worst full years were averaged to determine what the maximum downside risk was for any given year. As you can see, the aggressive portfolio had a higher rate of return but also a greater risk of loss. And, the aggressive portfolio also had the highest beta.

FIGURE 8-5 Picking your portfolio chart.

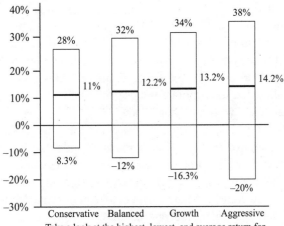

Take a look at the highest, lowest, and average return for the following sample core portfolios. The more return required, the more volatility endured.

FIGURE 8-6   Core portfolio 1—conservative.

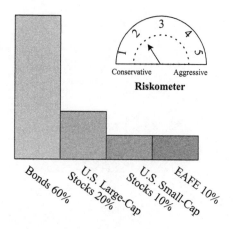

Total rate of return since 1970: 11%
Beta: 0.48%
Average 4 worst quarters: –6%
Average 4 worst years: –8.3%

FIGURE 8-7   Core portfolio 2—balanced.

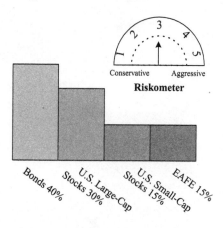

Total rate of return since 1970: 12.2%
Beta: 0.65%
Average 4 worst quarters: –8.9%
Average 4 worst years: –12%

FIGURE 8-8   Core portfolio 3—Growth.

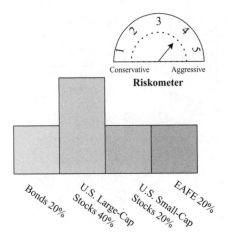

Total rate of return since 1970: 13.2%
Beta: 0.82%
Average 4 worst quarters: –12.22%
Average 4 worst years: –16.3%

FIGURE 8-9   Core portfolio 4—aggressive.

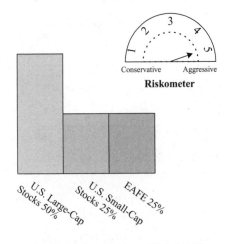

Total rate of return since 1970: 14.2%
Beta: 0.99%
Average 4 worst quarters: –15.6%
Average 4 worst years: –20%

Beta measures a stock's or portfolio's volatility compared with the market as a whole. The Standard & Poor's 500 is used as the benchmark (1.0) for measuring the beta of a stock or portfolio. A beta of 1.1 indicates that your stock is 10% more volatile than the market. A beta of .9 indicates that your stock is 10% less volatile than the market.

In a perfect world, you want a portfolio with the highest rate of return but the lowest beta. However, in reality, what you want is a portfolio with a reasonable rate of return that helps you meet your financial goals and a beta that you can sleep with. The U.S. large-cap and small-cap should be equally weighted between growth and value.

Now it's time to make your own asset allocations.

Refer to your 401(k) plan's menu of investment options or asset classes they offer and select those by percentage that will create the portfolio mix you desire. Start by deciding how much of your portfolio you want to be the "core" or bedrock of your investment plan. Then decide what percentage of the "core" should be stocks or bonds. And then decide how to allocate the stock portion between "value" and "growth" and how much should be invested in high quality international equities. In some 401(k) plans, there may actually be one or two "core" equity mutual funds that already include both value and growth styles. This is the simple way to diversify among both equity styles. For the remaining portion of your assets outside the "core," consider some of the other more aggressive investment options available like emerging market debt or emerging country stocks, or high-yield bonds, or even your own company's stock. Finally, don't forget to decide how the bond portion of the "core" should be invested—in either high-quality corporate bond mutual funds or government bond funds.

Congratulations—you've just created a diversified portfolio, consisting of a "core" allocation in stocks and bonds, along with a more aggressive, but limited portion of your 401(k) dollars!

C H A P T E R

KNOW WHERE TO GET HELP

Online Aids

EMPLOYERS ARE NOW BEGINNING TO MAKE it possible for employees to enroll in their benefit plans online. Online enrollment reduces miscommunications and costs and helps employees make the right choices. It also reduces the time your HR department spends processing enrollment forms.

401(k) Calculator

Benefit Software Inc. (www.bsiweb.com) offers a customizable online 401(k) calculator programmed with the federal maximum benefit and contribution limits, plus the Social Security and Medicare tax rates. It is designed to help employees model their contributions and evaluate the pocketbook effect of various savings strategies. By specifying the growth rate and assumptions such as annual gross pay, expected salary increases, annual 401(k) contributions, and years until retirement, employees can project the future value of their accounts. It also allows workers age 50 and up to take advantage of the catch-up rules enacted last year.

Larry DuBois, president of Benefit Software, explains that the calculator, when used with the company's Fringe Facts Online program, can also produce a statement that projects how much the worker could be saving.

Investment Company Institute

The Investment Company Institute (ICI) is a national association founded in 1940, whose membership includes 9,064 mutual funds, 485 closed-end funds, and six sponsors of unit investment trusts. Its mutual fund members represent nearly 89 million individual shareholders and manage approximately $7 trillion. The ICI "represents its members and their shareholders in matters of legislation, regulation, taxation, public information, economic and policy research, business operations, and statistics. ICI seeks to enhance public understanding of the investment company business, to serve the public interest by encouraging adherence to the highest ethical standards by all segments of the industry, and to promote the interests of fund shareholders." Web site: **www.ici.org**.

Profit Sharing/401(k) Council of America

The Profit Sharing/401(k) Council of America (PSCA) is a nonprofit association advocating increased retirement security through profit sharing, 401(k), and related defined contribution programs.
10 S. Riverside Plaza, Suite 1610
Chicago, IL 60606
Phone: 312 441-8550
Fax: 312 441-8559
E-mail: psca@psca.org
Web site: **www.psca.org**

Consulting an Advisor

Not everyone loves the Internet; there are still some people who would rather speak to someone personally.

We're not saying you can't do this on your own; but, given the com-

FIGURE 9-1   Getting help from an advisor.

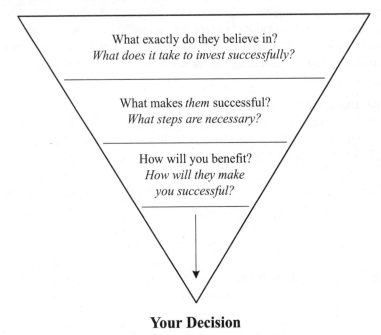

What exactly do they believe in?
What does it take to invest successfully?

What makes *them* successful?
What steps are necessary?

How will you benefit?
*How will they make
you successful?*

Your Decision

This inverted pyramid shows investors what questions
they need to ask before picking an advisor.

plexity of everything you've just read, it seems logical that you might find it a bit easier to consult a qualified financial advisor, someone who understands your overall personal situation and how it might best be served by your 401(k) investment.

The Department of Labor has recently issued an advisory opinion that should open the door for independent financial advisors to become more involved with 401(k) plan participants. The opinion gives companies the authority, without first seeking government approval, to hire independent firms to provide financial advice to individual investors and manage their 401(k) plans.

What can you do to be prepared before you meet with an advisor and what should you expect from one?

Before you interview investment advisors, spend some time redefining your personal investment profile—your investment attitude, objectives, and time frames. Be sure to include your family members in planning discussions, so their expectations will be in line with your goals. Develop a list of important issues and questions that might indicate areas of expertise to look for.

It's the advisor's job to help you create an overall plan (investment policy statement) to guide your lifelong investment decisions. This comprehensive plan calculates an individual's needed and expected rates of return on his or her portfolio, outlines what to do in extreme market conditions, measures risk and volatility, and measures costs incurred in a portfolio and attempts to minimize them.

> It's the advisor's job to help you create an overall plan (investment policy statement) to guide your lifelong investment decisions.

The advisor can help you determine whether or not your investment philosophy is actually in line with the return expected from your 401(k) mix. The goal is to set out the discipline of the process so no one has to worry that there will be misunderstandings down the road when sudden and unexpected changes occur in the financial world. If you don't have a method by which you will measure your success, then you subject yourself to external forces: comparing against the S&P 500, your friend's return, the top mutual funds, *Money* magazine, or how you feel at the moment.

The advisor should have a background in defined contribution plans. You may find that many advisors, stockbrokers, and money managers avoid 401(k) plan participants because they don't make any money selling products. Some advisors will work with you for a fee. They should provide you with an agreement that outlines expectations for the relationship, the roles each party will fulfill, and what each is accountable for. Establishing an agreement can help eliminate confusion, unmet expectations, and frustration.

Hiring an advisor doesn't mean you must give up all control. The exact role an advisor plays in your individual investment process is up to you. You may opt for an advisor who analyzes your financial condition, strategizes with you on the best path to take in the future, and then sends you on your way—in other words, educates you and then empowers you to take action on your own. The more hands-on help you want,

the more it will cost, but an ongoing relationship may be worth it.
Here are some key factors to research and consider:

- **Reputation.** How many accounts does the advisor/firm have
  and how many have been brought in over the last five years?
  How many have been lost? How big is the firm, both in terms
  of people and assets under management? Bigger is not necessarily better. Ask the advisor to provide three references. Fee-
  based advisors generally don't mind at all if you ask for references from current clients.
- **Investment Strategy.** Does the advisor have a well-defined,
  consistently applied investment process? What are the advisor's
  primary sources of research? Who participates in the investment decisions? How are tax considerations factored into the
  investment process?
- **Account Management.** How does the advisor rate in client
  service?

The Financial Advisor Community

Think of the variety of professionals selling investments and advice as
being like different divisions of the armed services. The Army, Navy,
Marine Corps, and Air Force all have a similar objective and often
even use the same type of equipment; they just carry out their missions
differently.

Many investors assume their brokers are well-trained money managers. This is not necessarily true. Anyone who can pass one six-hour
test administered by the National Association of Securities Dealers can
become a broker. Full-service broker-dealers have relationships with a
universe of money managers and large research departments.

Stockbrokers believe they're at the top of the pecking order; bank
representatives believe they sell on hallowed ground; and fee-only advisors sense they are close to nirvana. Yet they all may be selling the same
exact investment product or offering the same service. Their joint mis-
sion is to help their clients successfully meet their financial goals.
Unfortunately, financial advisors with the highest marks and those with

the worst records are all known by the same title. The public can't tell who is competent and who is not, so how does an investor choose?

Financial Planners

This group can be either advisors or brokers, depending on whether they specialize in financial planning; and can charge fees for services and/or commissions. They can provide you with for-fee or free financial planning reports—which can cost hundreds, or thousands, of dollars.

For a fee, consultants in many large firms can help you establish your investment objectives, do the research and due diligence needed to find an appropriate money manager or the right mutual funds for you, and—most important—provide sophisticated monitoring and review of the money manager who is managing your account.

You still need to be aware that more than 200,000 women and men call themselves financial planners, including accountants, attorneys, stockbrokers, insurance agents, self-styled money managers, credit counselors, and the Internet junkie down the street. But only a small number of these are registered certified financial planners, a designation that guarantees a person has passed a rigorous set of tests in all areas of personal finance (investing, retirement and estate planning, taxes, insurance, and more) and has at least three years of experience in the field.

Certified Financial Planner: To earn this designation, candidates must pass a comprehensive, 10-hour examination given by the Denver-based Certified Financial Planner Board of Standards. Every two years after receiving their degrees, CFPs must complete 30 hours of continuing education to remain certified. Most CFPs are self-employed. Others are brokers, accountants, lawyers, or insurance agents. Some are *fee-only*, meaning they charge a set fee for advice or to develop a plan. Others also charge commissions for selling products.

The Certified Financial Planner Board of Standards has a public responsibility as a standard-setting organization. Part of that responsibility is to let the public know that they can trust CFP professionals to adhere to their code of ethics, that there is an enforcement method for those who violate that code and a process in place to really hold CFPs accountable. To keep up with industry trends, practice standards are reviewed and updated every five years. The board disciplines CFPs for unethical conduct, by issuing a letter of admonition, suspending them, or revoking their CFP designation. Some cases also involve disciplinary action taken by the National Association of Securities Dealers.

Chartered Financial Consultant: ChFCs offer comprehensive financial planning services. They must take 10 courses on financial planning topics and pass 10 two-hour exams prepared by The American College in Bryn Mawr, PA. ChFCs must also complete 60 hours of continuing education every two years. Typically, they charge a flat fee for developing a financial plan, but they can also charge commissions.

CPA/PFS (Certified Public Accountant/Personal Financial Specialist): This designation is bestowed by the American Institute of Certified Public Accountants (based in New York) on CPAs who pass an exam and meet work-experience requirements. A PFS must pass a comprehensive exam given by the American Institute of Certified Public Accountants and perform a designated number of hours of personal financial planning services and continuing education.

Chartered Financial Analyst: A CFA is viewed as the most prestigious credential in the investment industry; however, it focuses on investment analysis rather than financial planning. Most specialize in securities analysis and provide investment advice. Many are personal or institutional money managers. Others manage portfolios for mutual funds, trust companies, or broker-dealers. CFA candidates must pass three exams over a minimum of three years administered by the Association for Investment Management and Research in Charlottesville, VA. Many portfolio managers who manage separate accounts are CFAs.

Registered Investment Advisor: RIAs must file an informational (ADV) form with the SEC annually and pay a one-time fee. It is important to note that the designation RIA does not necessarily mean that the person is qualified to manage your money, nor that he or she has gone through an extraordinary educational course. It is just that to charge fees, he or she must be registered with the SEC as an RIA. By law, these advisors must give you Part II of the ADV Form, which covers fee structure, financial services, and investment strategy. But you will also want to see Part I and the accompanying schedules, which detail disciplinary actions, education, account custody arrangements, and the number of clients the advisor counsels.

Full-Service Brokers

Most full-service stockbrokers solicit business and are paid by commissions. "Full-service" means they offer a wider variety of financial products. Products they offer include stocks, bonds, derivatives, annuities, and insurance. They also offer investment advice and research. Most full-service brokers are moving in the direction of charging fees.

Many stockbrokers attempt to add value by following traditional investment strategies such as trying to pick exceptional mutual funds—or predicting which way the market's going. Remember earlier chapters, just a reminder no one can do that successfully.

Active strategies entail investigation and analysis expenses, and these judgment calls may also involve the acceptance of a degree of diversifiable risk. The extra costs and risks can be substantial and must be justified by realistically evaluated return expectations. The national full service firms, most of whom are based in New York, are moving away from being paid on a transaction basis and toward charging fees for advice.

Discount Brokers

Discount brokerages usually don't offer the full range of services or research provided by full-service brokers. Most *do not* offer advice; they simply transact trades. Because they manage fewer products than their full-service counterparts, discounters charge considerably lower fees. Discounters also may offer online computerized order entry services. Those that have live brokers generally pay them a set salary to execute trades. The brokers don't solicit and aren't paid commissions. Discount brokerages make money by doing business in volume, competing mostly on price and reliability of service. If they have the lowest prices and the best service, they get the most trades. But, they also provide the least amount of advice.

Bank Investment Representatives

This is like having a "broker-in-the-bank." For decades, consumers have listed banks as the most trusted source of financial products and advice. The primary reason: bank savings and CDs are backed by the FDIC. Traditional bankers, however, knew little about investments, financial planning, or diversification; and bank employees were trained basically in making loans, taking deposits, and issuing credit cards.

Then a few years ago, banks decided to cross over the line and offer investments through subsidiaries or affiliates, since banks are prohibited from offering investments directly. These bank affiliate advisors have the same securities licenses as other brokers, and many have gone through traditional Wall Street training programs. However, not many have been trained in 401(k) plan investing.

Investment Management Consultants

Pure investment management consultants normally work for Wall Street firms and specialize in consulting with investors about their investments. They help investors set financial goals and come up with comprehensive plans, rather than simply trying to sell particular investments. They charge fees for services rather than charging commissions on transactions.

They take a much broader approach and maintain a macro perspective of global, small cap, and large cap equities. They must have three years of verifiable experience and pass a course to attain the designation of Certified Investment Management Analyst (CIMA), awarded by the Investment Management Consultants Association.

Independent Fee-Only Financial Advisors

There are various types of advisors, and many are very good. They act in ways that are similar to the big Wall Street firms' investment management consultants. Like investment management consultants, these advisors have no incentive to sell you a financial product for a commission. They still have access to all the mutual fund vendors and meet with representatives of many mutual fund companies.

Many of these financial advisors have formed alliances with professionals in related fields, set up formalized networking relationships with existing planners, estate planners, CPAs, state attorneys, and/or insurance specialists. The following professional organizations will provide you with select lists of financial planners in your area who understand 401(k) plans. Here also are some online directories:

National Association of Personal Financial Advisors (NAPFA)
1-888-FEE-ONLY
www.napfa.org
NAPFA has a membership of fee-only financial planners.
Membership: 750

The Financial Planning Association (FPA)
1-800-282-PLAN
www.fpanet.org
The Institute of Certified Financial Planners and the International Association for Financial Planning unified on January 1, 2000 to become the FPA.
Membership: 30,000

American Institute of Certified Public Accountants
Personal Financial Planning Division
1-800-862-4272
www.aicpa.org
AICPA's personal financial planning division is made up of CPAs who have earned a Personal Financial Specialist designation. Membership: 7,000

How Do Advisors Get Paid?
Different advisors charge differently. Some charge a commission; some charge a fee. If advisors are fee-based, they will generally charge a flat fee or a fee based on the amount of assets that you have and that they are giving advice on. Over the long run, you're going to be better off working with advisors who charge a flat fee. You can take their advice and implement it yourself. Some advisors charge the same fee as others but provide a lot less, so the real struggle is finding an advisor who will give you what you need and charge the right amount.

> Many of the major fund companies are now coming out with new retirement shares with different expense ratios, but they are specifically designated for 401(k) plans.

Most mutual funds in 401(k) plans today are sold without any fees or commissions to the participants. But, if an advisor is tied into the plan, he may be receiving a form of ongoing payment from the 12b fees (see Glossary) inside the fund.

Investment advisors do not have to share the revenue with anyone else when they charge for services. They typically charge an annual asset fee based on a graduated schedule. Ask if your investment advisor receives any other fees when working with a fund manager.

Many of the major fund companies are now coming out with new retirement shares with different expense ratios, but they are specifically designated for 401(k) plans. By waiving the front end load, they can now increase the fees to the broker; the slightly higher expense ratio allows the broker to be paid enough to continue to provide services to the participants, but yet there is no front end sales charge and there is no continued deferred sales charge (CDSC—back end fee). Go to your 401(k) plan's mutual fund Web site to get a full description.

It's still up to you to do your homework. You really need to establish a list of criteria for your specific needs. Ask the appropriate questions and, if any answer is unacceptable, go on to the next advisor. Take your time. Don't be pressured. Try to find the right person, someone who you're comfortable with and who will be on your side.

The highest probability of success comes from:

- Good communications
- Understanding 401(k) plan rules
- Knowing your appropriate return
- Understanding the different investments
- Having a strategy that works, and one that fits with your own personal temperament

The form on the next two pages, "the advisor selector," was created by Susan Latremoille, The Latremoille Group Vice President and Portfolio Manager, RBC Investments Inc. This advisor selector will help you make the right decision in choosing the advisor most appropriate for your needs.

The Advisor Selector

	1	2	3	4	5	6	7	8	9	10	
The organization is not well known or does not have a reputationi in the 401(k) field.											The organization is highly regarded and has a fine reputation in managing portfolios for individuals like me.
The advisor is more interested in trying to sell me on his/her proposal.											The advisor is interested in spending time with me to help me understand my unique investment goals and needs
I am not sure whom I will be dealing with in the future.											The advisor is supported by a team of associates who each play a role in supporting me in achieving my goals.
I don't know how many staff members my advisor employs and the number of clients they serve.											I know the number of clients and staff that the advisor has in his or her practice.
I am not sure how my advisor intends to work with me on an ongoing basis.											The advisor has clearly articulated their process of how we will work together.
I am not totally sure that this advisor will be right for me over the long term.											I am confident that I will enjoy working with this advisor and their team in the years ahead.
I am not sure that this advisor is approachable on other financially related matters.											I feel that I can approach the advisor with any issue of a financial nature.
There are parts of the plan that I do not understand and are confusing to me.											I can easily understand allo aspects of the plan that I have received.
The investment plan does not deal with my various needs outside my retirement assests.											The investment plan incorporates all of my various needs to one cohesive strategy, including asset.
The investment plan does not consider how my retirement assets are currently managed.											The investment plan takes into consideration how my retirement assets are currently managed.
There is no evidence of attention to tax efficiency in the investment plan.											The investment plan emphasizes tex efficiency in my portfolio.

The Advisor Selector (Continued)

	1	2	3	4	5	6	7	8	9	10	
I am not sure that I know all the costs associated with managing my portfolio.											I am fully aware of all fees and costs associated with managing my portfolio.
I am not sure what value will be created for the money that I will be paying to have my portfolio managed.											I feel that I will receive value from the money that I am paying for the management of my portfolio.
I do not know what the overall asset mix and allocation will be in my portfolio.											I know what the asset mix and allocation will be in my portfolio.
I have some hesitation about selecting this advisor to work with me.											I feel totally confident about selecting this advisor to work with me.
Add column totals											Your score:

Which advisor makes me feel most comfortable about handling my investment portfolio? Why?

My first reaction is to hire: _____

10

KNOW HOW TO GET YOUR MONEY OUT SAFELY

The Distribution Rules

BECAUSE OF TAX IMPLICATIONS AND INFLATION, how you take distributions from your retirement funds at termination of your employment or the plan will be more important than how you put the money in! You have five possible options for distributing monies from your 401(k) plan:

1. Request a lump-sum distribution.
2. Roll your money over into an IRA.
3. Buy an annuity.
4. Request minimum or periodic distributions.
5. Leave your money in the plan, as long as the plan allows it.

Nothing beats the ability to have your money continue to grow, tax-deferred, until you need or want it. Tax-deferred compounding is truly the eighth wonder of the world; but eventually, *all good things must come to an end.*

Lump-Sum Distributions

A lump-sum distribution is a distribution from a qualified retirement plan of the entire sum of a participant's balance to a participant within a single taxable year. A lump-sum distribution will allow the recipient under current law to receive special tax treatment designed to reduce the dramatic impact of

> A lump-sum distribution will allow the recipient under current law to receive special tax treatment designed to reduce the dramatic impact of this kind of distribution.

this kind of distribution. The IRS allows you to pay the tax as if you had spread out the distribution over a 10-year period. The reason for their generosity is that they are getting your money up front, and they don't have to wait for the taxes to dribble in over the next 30 years.

To qualify as a lump-sum distribution, the payment must be made for one of the following reasons:

- The employee dies.
- The employee reaches age 59½.
- The employee separates from the employer (through retirement, a job change, or termination).
- The employee becomes disabled (self-employed individuals only).

There are a variety of specific conditions associated with the lump-sum distribution rules, such as your distribution must qualify as a lump-sum distribution (meaning that it includes all taxable money from all plans), you must be age 59½ or over, and you must have participated in the 401(k) plan for five or more taxable years before the distribution. The details of these regulations are beyond the scope of this book and you should discuss them with a qualified tax practitioner.

Tax-Free Rollovers

Another type of distribution that is afforded favorable tax treatment is a *rollover* of your pre-tax contributions and investment earnings from a 401(k), IRA, or other qualified retirement plan (403[b], 457 pension plan, profit-sharing plan, or employee stock ownership plan [ESOP]) into another qualified plan. Many people equate the term "rollover" with IRAs and are under the misconception that another IRA can be the only destination. But, if the plan sponsor permits it, the new law allows rollovers into a 403(b), a 457, and other qualified plans.

In order to be treated as a *tax-free* rollover, the distribution must be a *qualifying distribution.* Such qualifying distributions may be either total or partial distributions, each of which is precisely defined according to certain conditions. However, most employers won't let you make a partial rollover of your plan money and keep the rest where it is.

You are generally eligible for a tax-free rollover at the time your employment ends, you become disabled, or you retire. Also, if you receive a distribution from a 401(k) as a surviving spouse, you can request a tax-free rollover into an IRA only.

> **If you do a rollover correctly, the amount rolled over will not be subject to taxes until you take out the money in the future. The earnings will also continue to accrue untaxed.**

If you do a rollover correctly, the amount rolled over will not be subject to taxes until you take out the money in the future. The earnings will also continue to accrue untaxed.

If you do it wrong, you'll pay some tax immediately and possibly a 10% early payment penalty *in addition to* income taxes. At worst, you'll forever lose your chance to defer taxes on this money. Since the rules governing rollovers to and from IRAs and 401(k)s are similar, but with some differences, always seek the help of a qualified tax professional.

The laws that govern distributions from 401(k)s and pension plans encourage rollovers so that this tax-deferred savings for retirement will be continued by workers. However, 60% of departing participants keep the money and pay the taxes rather than rolling it over.

If you are going to a new employer that has a 401(k) plan, you should be able to roll over your existing 401(k) money into that plan. In the event that you do, your rollover money is kept separate from any new money contributed. However, check out your new employer's plan rules before making your rollover decision. Some companies will require you to be eligible to participate before you can roll money in, while others will let you make a rollover before you're eligible to contribute to their plan. Your new employer is not required to accept rollovers, and not all employers do.

Your plan sponsor is required to advise you of your options in writing, but there are generally two.

Direct Rollover. A *direct* rollover is technically referred to as a "trustee-to-trustee" transfer. In other words, you never receive a check. Usually, when you request this type of rollover, your distribution is wire-transferred directly to your new plan's trustee.

If you leave your employment with a plan balance of more than $1,000, but not more than $5,000 (not including money that you rolled in from another plan), and you don't elect a distribution option, your plan must automatically roll over any distribution to an IRA on your behalf. Your plan sponsor gets to choose the IRA provider and how your money gets invested in that IRA, subject to certain guidelines that will be issued by the government. You now have a rollover IRA, also known as a *conduit* IRA. If you keep this separated from all of your other IRAs and don't add any new contributions to it, you will preserve the right to roll it into a 401(k) plan in the future.

Regular Rollover. If you request a *regular* rollover, the trustee of the plan will send you a check made payable to you. By law, the trustee is required to withhold 20% of your money and pay it to the federal government. The money you receive must be deposited into another qualified retirement plan within 60 days to avoid being taxed as income. The 60 days begins when the check arrives. (The IRS is allowed to waive the 60-day rule only in cases of natural disaster, hospitalization, or "other similar hardship.")

Say you're not yet re-employed and you're not sure what to do about the $10,000 sitting in your 401(k), so you opt for a regular rollover. As a result, you're going to get a check made out to you for $8,000. The other $2,000 (20%) goes *automatically* to the federal government for income tax. Then you find a new employer and put the $8,000 back into a tax-deferred account before 60 days expire. However, you'll have to wait until you file your income taxes to get a refund for the $2,000 that was withheld. In other words, you just loaned Uncle Sam $2,000 interest-free for several months. Plus, because the total distribution was $10,000, but you rolled over only $8,000, the other $2,000 gets treated as income and you pay tax on that amount.

There is a form you can sign at the time of the distribution saying you are exempt from the 20% withholding; but, if you don't make a qualified rollover within the 60 days, for whatever reason, you'll be responsible for the income tax and very possibly also some interest and penalties from the date of distribution until the time you file your income tax forms.

Here's what can be rolled over:

- Pre-tax contributions and their investment earnings.
- All contributions made by your employer, such as matching and profit-sharing contributions, that are fully vested, as well as the earnings on those contributions.
- Any funds in your current 401(k) plan that were rolled over from a previous employer and the earnings on these amounts.
- After-tax contributions and their investment earnings *only* to another qualified 401(k) or IRA. Some other special rules apply, such as, if you move this money to another employer's plan, you must use the *direct rollover* method (trustee-to-trustee transfer). Your new employer or the IRA provider must be willing and able to accept the after-tax money and to maintain separate accounting for it.
- Distributions from pension plans and ESOPs.

Here's what can't be rolled over:

- If you have an outstanding loan balance against your plan when you leave the company, it is considered a payment to you, technically called a "deemed distribution." You can't roll over an outstanding loan balance and continue loan payments.
- If you have company stock and your employer distributes shares instead of cash, you'll have a challenge rolling it over. Virtually no new 401(k) trustees will accept the stock as a rollover, and most financial institutions won't either. Some brokerage firms will take your rollover in shares. Try to get your company to cash you out instead.

Caution: If you choose an IRA for your rollover, check out the IRA administrator's minimum deposits. Some banks, brokerages, and insurance companies require a minimum of $1,000 to $10,000 before you can open an IRA. Others charge a hefty fee for small accounts. It doesn't make much sense rolling over $1,000 and being charged a fee of $30 a year (3%) for administration.

If you're rolling over both pre-tax and after-tax money, you need to be sure that your IRA provider can handle the separate accounting that's required. Otherwise, you may have to establish two accounts—one for the pre-tax money and all the earnings and another for your after-tax contributions.

If you roll your money over to an IRA, there are more than 8,500 retail mutual funds available, so an IRA rollover will give you more investment choices, including separate account management. The trustee will help you make the proper decision about timing and amounts so that you don't run afoul of the IRS rules. You will be taxed on funds as you withdraw them, but what you don't withdraw will continue to compound, tax-deferred, within the IRA. With the IRA, you also have easy access to your money or, if you have enough retirement income from Social Security and your pension, you can leave the money in your account until you must begin withdrawals at age 70½.

Annuities

You can take your distribution in the form of an *annuity*—a series of payments meant to last your lifetime or that of you and your beneficiary. An annuity guarantees that you will not run out of income during your lifetime. But, it offers no guarantee against your greatest enemy in retirement—inflation. It does not make adjustments for the cost of living. You can also first roll your 401(k) proceeds into an IRA, and then purchase an annuity. There are many types of annuities and you may want to obtain help from a professional in selecting the one best suited to your needs.

> An annuity guarantees that you will not run out of income during your lifetime. But, it offers no guarantee against your greatest enemy in retirement—inflation.

Minimum Distributions

Because retirees are generally living longer, they are rarely taking their money out in large distributions. It's smart to spread that money out; but, you must begin taking at least a minimum distribution from your plan by April 1 following the year in which you reach age 70½. The IRS determines what the minimum amount is that you must withdraw each year, based on life-expectancy tables.

There used to be two methods to calculate your minimum distributions, the *term-certain* method and the *recalculation* method. Before you could figure out which method would be best, you'd have to decide who the beneficiary of your plan would be. The calculations were complicated and, if you changed your beneficiary, it could seriously complicate your distribution planning. Fortunately, there are new, simplified rules for minimum required distributions.

The New Minimum Distribution Incidental Benefit Table calculates life expectancy as if your beneficiary is 10 years younger than you. Because of these new tables, there's no deadline to name a beneficiary. You get to use the new uniform life-expectancy table whether or not you've named a beneficiary. And you can change your beneficiary at any time without (usually) worrying about having to recalculate the distribution because of the change.

The beneficiary uses his or her own life expectancy to figure required distributions after your death. If there is more than one beneficiary, the age of the oldest is used to figure the distribution. A spouse gets a special advantage and doesn't have to begin taking distributions until the year in which you would have turned 70½. Heirs get up to five years to withdraw money after your death. If you die before you've begun your required minimum distributions and you have not yet named a beneficiary, your spouse or heirs will have up to five years to withdraw the money and pay the taxes. Spousal benefits can only be waived with their consent. If you are concerned about this, consult an attorney.

Section 72(t) Distributions

Section 72(t) of the IRS code is a well-kept secret. It allows periodic distributions without penalty prior to age 59½ based upon IRS-approved calculations of "substantially equal payments." The major fact to keep in mind is you must continue receiving these equal payments for at least five years or until you reach age 59½, whichever is longer. So, if you're 57 years old, you must take payments until age 62.

All IRA and 403(b) account owners are eligible at any time for any reason. Participants in a 401(k) plan are eligible only after separation from service (fired or quit), death (and the beneficiary will receive the payments), or total disability. According to the IRS, you must meet a special definition of "disability" by virtue of being unable to "engage in any substantial gainful activity by reason of a medically determinable physical or mental impairment which can be expected to result in death or to be of long-continued and indefinite duration."

This is worthwhile to consider only if you have a large account, because the payments are based upon your life expectancy and, if you are in your 40s, they could be quite small. But remember, by beginning distributions at a young age, you forego the tax-deferred compounding.

Once the distributions have begun, you are locked in. If the payment scheduled is modified for any reason other than a disability or death before you meet the above criterion, the IRS will impose that 10% penalty plus interest, and it will be retroactive.

Leave Your Money in the Plan

Most of the time, you don't have to take your money out of your old employer's plan when you terminate employment. Former employers are required by law to let you leave your money in their 401(k) plans if your balance is above $5,000.

Maybe you're unsure about your new employer's future. Maybe you prefer the investment options in your old employer's plan. Perhaps your old employer's plan does not charge an annual maintenance fee. (A rollover IRA or a new employer's plan might have such a fee.) Or, you just don't know what to do. You should probably leave it where it is as an interim measure until you've had time to think about it. That way, you continue to shelter your contributions and earnings from taxes. However, forget about making new contributions to your plan.

> **Most of the time, you don't have to take your money out of your old employer's plan when you terminate employment.**

Also, if you have an outstanding loan from your plan and can't afford to fully repay it all at once, by leaving your account intact, you could continue to make your loan payments, if your former employer is agreeable.

If your employer will allow you to leave the money in the account, he or she may also allow you to take the money out in installment payouts. Taxes will be due annually on the payouts you receive, so this system takes some planning.

Loans

A way of accessing your retirement assets while still employed is by borrowing against them. Although about 83% of all 401(k) plans offer loans, many small companies just can't afford to add a loan feature to their 401(k) plan because of the high cost of administering it. If the plan does permit loans, the plan sponsor can determine the restrictions. *Note:* If you're no longer an employee, but have left your money in your previous employer's plan, you won't be able to get a loan on your old account.

Listed here are just basic guidelines, but many plans do adopt them, because it's easier than trying to set their own guidelines and trying to please everyone. Keep in mind that individual plans can add to this list.

Many plans stipulate that your loan be used only for hardship reasons:

- To pay education expenses (for yourself, your spouse, or a child)
- To prevent eviction from your home
- To pay unreimbursed medical expenses
- To buy a first-time residence (a single-family home, a condominium, a co-op, or even a mobile home)

So, if you're thinking about borrowing, first check to see if it's allowed in your plan. Ask for a copy of the plan's loan program and read the fine print. If the plan allows loans, they are usually easy to obtain because no credit check is necessary. If you've got the money in your account, they'll usually loan it to you so long as your reason fits the loan criteria, unless they need spousal consent and your spouse is unwilling to give it.

When the loan is approved, there is paperwork to be signed. You may be borrowing money from yourself, but you're entering into a legal and binding agreement with the plan trustee. Before you sign anything, read it through to make sure you understand it.

You'll have to complete a legal document called a *promissory note* that says, "I do hereby promise to repay this loan." The promissory note states the amount of the loan, the interest rate, the duration of the loan, and the terms of repayment. If you're married, your spouse may have to give consent. Your spouse is not cosigning for the loan, just consenting to it. Check if your plan's rules require spousal consent before you request the loan.

How much can you borrow?

First, how much do you have in the plan? You can borrow up to half your *vested* account balance, up to a maximum of $50,000. Many plans specify a minimum amount of at least $1,000 as well (because of the paperwork). Your employer can tighten up on these rules, but most do not. While there is no limit on the number of times you can borrow against your plan, most plans allow only one outstanding loan at a time.

And for how long?

Many 401(k) plans allow extended-term loans (for 15, 20, or even 30 years) for the purchase of a primary residence. But, say you take a 20-year, $20,000 loan from your 401(k) account for the down payment, what's the likelihood of your staying at that company for the next 20 years? How will you pay back that 20-year, $20,000 loan when you leave the company? If you're saving to buy a home, there may be better alternative savings vehicles.

How much will it cost?

Partly to discourage plan participants from taking loans, most plans charge a fee. This charge is usually levied by the record keeper to off-set internal expenses.

You'll pay perhaps $25 to $75 or more to set up the loan and $10 to $50 every year to administer it. Sometimes the loan fee is deducted from the loan proceeds. So, in effect, you're financing the loan fee in addition to the loan. The other way you might pay the loan fee is to have it automatically deducted from your account.

Plans must charge the current market interest rate, equiva-

> **Plans must charge the current market interest rate, equivalent to what you would be charged at the local bank. No sweetheart deals here, even if it is your own money.**

lent to what you would be charged at the local bank. No sweetheart deals here, even if it is your own money. The transaction must be considered at arm's length, meaning it would pass muster with the Department of Labor as being legitimate. The interest rate is usually one or two percentage points above the prime rate (the same as the loan rate available to a bank's best customer). This rate is fixed over the life of your loan, but could change for future loans due to changes in the prime rate.

The good news is that the interest that you're paying will go right into your 401(k) account along with the amount you're paying back each paycheck. The bad news is that the interest on a 401(k) loan is not deductible, even it you use it to purchase a home.

Repayment

Most companies make it easy for you to pay back the loan by doing payroll deductions. The record keeper usually takes your loan repayments directly from your paycheck after taxes. Check your pay stub and your loan agreement to confirm the deductions are the right amounts. Then check your loan statements to make sure the principal portions of these amounts reduce your outstanding balance. When the loan is repaid, check that the plan administrator stops deducting loan payments.

If you can't do payroll deductions, you'll be required to make at least quarterly payments to the plan trustee. You can pay off the entire loan before it's due, but don't count on the manager letting you increase principal payments along the way, like you might do with a mortgage, because of the administrative hassle.

What if you can't pay back the loan?

The IRS says that if you fail to pay back the loan, you'll be in default. In other words, the outstanding balance will be treated as if you withdrew the money before retirement. You'll pay federal and state income taxes on this money, and possibly the 10% early withdrawal penalty. So, if you run into a cash-flow problem and you can't repay your loan, ask your manager (the plan administrator) if you can take advantage of the 90-day IRS grace period.

If you leave your employer for any reason and you have an outstanding loan, in most cases you need to repay it immediately. If you can't, the plan sponsor may allow you to maintain your account and continue making your loan payments even though you are no longer an employee. Otherwise, the outstanding loan is considered a premature withdrawal. The record keeper must send you a 1099R and copy the IRS, stating that you've taken a distribution from your retirement plan. You'll owe taxes on the outstanding amount left on the loan. If you're under age 59½, you'll owe a 10% penalty as well.

How does it affect your 401(k) investments?

When you take out a loan, the record keeper withdraws money from your account and writes you a check. Since the money is coming out of your investment funds, make sure you know which fund(s) the record keeper has deducted your loan from. Most of the money will come from those funds that have the largest balances. Some plans allow you to direct that loan proceeds be taken out of a particular fund.

Your loan repayments may not necessarily go back into the funds you withdrew from. This is easily solved. Just rebalance your future contributions according to where you want your loan payments and paycheck deductions going.

Generally it is not a good idea to borrow from your 401(k) plan.

One big issue that is often overlooked is the "double taxation" on loans. The dollars you're contributing to the 401(k) are going into the plan pre-tax. Now you take those dollars out in the form of a loan, but the dollars you're using to pay back the loan are being taxed before you use them to pay off the loan. Then, 20 or so years from now, when you begin to withdraw retirement distributions from your account, you're going to be required to pay income tax on all of your withdrawals, including those after-tax dollars you used to repay your loan and interest.

> Don't use your 401(k) plan as a rainy-day savings fund for emergencies!

Don't use your 401(k) plan as a rainy-day savings fund for emergencies! Your emergency might not qualify for a loan; and then you will have to pay taxes and penalties for a withdrawal. Plus, it will probably take two to six weeks or more for the plan administrator to get you a check. Your emergency might not wait that long!

Some 401(k) plans allow you to buy whole life, variable life, or flexible life insurance with your 401(k) contributions. Wrapping up insurance inside a 401(k) plan makes little sense, especially when the expense charges are considerably more than similar investments.

First of all, life insurance is not an investment. Second, life insurance—even policies that offer an investment component, such as variable life insurance—is already tax-sheltered. You don't pay taxes on it. If you die, your beneficiary receives the settlement and won't owe income taxes on it.

If you need life insurance, buy pure life insurance coverage (insurance that is only insurance and that builds no cash value). Buy term life insurance outside your 401(k) and invest to accumulate inside your 401(k).

What about saving for your children's education? Two types of much more appropriate *qualified state tuition plans* (QSTPs) exist—prepaid tuition plans and higher education savings account plans (a.k.a. Section 529 plans). Section 529 plans are very flexible. About 43 states now (but all states will eventually) sponsor them; some, such as Missouri and New York, will give you a state income tax deduction if you live in that state. As with education savings accounts, distributions are tax-free. A minor difference between the two is that 529s can be used only for college and graduate school expenses.

Withdrawing from Your Retirement Plan

The IRS says that you get access to your retirement funds without employment termination or retirement, but you will pay taxes and a penalty. Your employer may allow three types of withdrawals:

- Hardship withdrawals
- Age-restricted withdrawals
- Withdrawals of after-tax contributions

Hardship Withdrawals

With the exception of loans, the only way that participants can access their plan monies is in the case of *hardship*. Many plans do not have a hardship provision, but if they do, the plan document must define what constitutes a hardship. The hardship provision imposes considerable administrative responsibilities, but makes plan participation more favorable, because employees feel that they have the ability to access their money in the event of an emergency.

A hardship withdrawal is still liable for taxes and, if you're not at least 59½, you'll owe a 10% penalty as well. (If you are in the 28% federal tax bracket and are liable for state taxes *and* you are under age 59½, you could owe over *40%* of your withdrawal in taxes and penalties.)

According to the IRS code that governs this, a plan may permit a hardship withdrawal only if:

- The withdrawal is *due* to an immediate and heavy financial need.
- The withdrawal is *necessary* to satisfy that need.

As an example, the IRS regulations state that the need to pay funeral expenses for a family member constitutes such a need, whereas the need to purchase a television does not.

Safe Harbor Tests Set Forth in the IRS Regulations

The IRS states that a hardship withdrawal will be considered for reasons of immediate and heavy financial need for any of the following situations:

- Certain medical (including funeral) expenses for the participants, spouses, or dependents
- Purchase of the participant's principal residence (but not for mortgage payments)
- Payment of tuition for the next semester or quarter of postsecondary education for the participants, spouses, or children or dependents
- Payments necessary to prevent eviction from a participant's principal residence or foreclosure

Only those conditions just mentioned will permit such a withdrawal. Other severe financial needs cannot justify a distribution.

It is the responsibility of the employer to determine whether the participant has demonstrated a true hardship.

The second part of the code requires the employer to determine whether the withdrawal is necessary to satisfy the need and does not exceed the amount needed to relieve the financial need. The employer is permitted to rely on a written representation by the participant that the withdrawal is necessary for the purposes stated earlier and that the need cannot be satisfied through:

- Reimbursement or compensation by insurance
- Liquidation of the employee's assets
- The employee's cessation of plan contributions
- Other loans from commercial sources at reasonable terms

In addition, the participants must have made all withdrawals and nontaxable loans available under all plans maintained by the employer.

Additional Caveats

The participant cannot contribute to the plan for the next six months after receipt of the hardship withdrawal.

When the participant resumes making contributions to the plan, the maximum contribution allowed in the first year is reduced by the amount of the elective contribution made in the year in which the hardship withdrawal was taken.

The participant may be very limited in what he or she can contribute the following year.

If the participant is married, his or her spouse may have to provide written consent for the hardship withdrawal.

Age-Restricted Withdrawals

The IRS says that when you've passed its early-retirement penalty age (age 59½), you may get access to your money, if your employer allows it. It is a good-news-bad-news situation. The bad news: your employer will withhold 20% until tax time. The good news: with age comes the benefit of escaping the 10% penalty.

The 10% penalty does not apply to distributions made to an employee after separation of service (fired or quit) after attaining age 55. To qualify for an exemption, you have to have been employed in your 55th year. You cannot take an early retirement at age 52 and then, in three years, start distributions from your plan and hope to use this method of distributions to avoid the penalty.

Withdrawals of After-Tax Contributions

About 40% of 401(k) plans let you make additional contributions with after-tax money in addition to your pre-tax contributions. But, if these additional savings need to be liquidated, the cost can be very expensive. You might want to consider other, more liquid, investments for your after-tax money.

Remember that a 401(k) withdrawal option is discretionary. In other words, the sponsor doesn't have to make it available to you. In fact, many 401(k) plans do not offer age 59½ or hardship withdrawals. And more companies are dropping the after-tax feature.

Qualified Domestic Relations Order

Through a Qualified Domestic Relations Order (QDRO), a court can decree the distribution of property (for example, retirement plan assets) for child support or alimony. The court can assign all or a portion of your plan benefits to a former spouse, child, or dependent. The court circumvents you entirely and goes right to the plan trustees.

The person who is now entitled to all or part of the 401(k) has some decisions to make. Taking it in a lump sum will trigger taxes on the payout, but not a penalty even if the recipient is under age 59½. Leaving it inside the plan will depend on the courts and the summary plan description. However, leaving it will not trigger taxes until the funds are distributed. Rolling it into an IRA is by far the best option, but is allowed only between spouses. No taxes will be due until the funds are distributed, and with an IRA there will be many investment choices available. If the recipient of the 401(k) is a child or dependent, any taxes due on the distribution must be paid by the owner of the 401(k) account.

Free Information

The IRS provides some specific tax information in publications that are free for the asking. The phone number to request forms and publications is 1-800-829-3676. Or download and print them from the Web site, **www.irs.gov**.

Here are the relevant documents:

- Publication 590, Individual Retirement Arrangements, which deals with the rollover rules (**www.irs.gov/pub/irs-pdf/p590.pdf**)
- Publication 575, Pension and Annuity Income, which deals with 401(k) distributions (**www.irs.gov/pub/irs-pdf/p575.pdf**)
- Publication 1565, Looking Out for #2: A Married Couple's Guide to Understanding Your Benefit Choices at Retirement From a Defined Contribution Plan.

PULLING IT ALL TOGETHER

HERE IS A QUICK CHECKLIST OF THE 10 STEPS all 401(k) participants must take immediately to secure their investments and any gains they have made so far.

1. Pay Yourself First

You cannot afford *not* to participate in your 401(k) plan! No matter what sacrifice you must make to do so, do so now! Pay yourself the same way you do Uncle Sam—mandatory and off the top. It might even reduce the amount of tax you pay.

2. Increase Your Contributions

Money invested inside your 401(k) grows tax-deferred and compounds exponentially. You should invest every dollar of the maximum pre-tax contribution allowed, to take the full advantage of these valuable benefits.

3. Take Full Advantage of Matching Contributions

Don't turn down free money! Make sure you are qualifying for the maximum of matched contributions. Read the fine print of your 401(k) summary plan description (SPD) to learn the terms and look for areas that could increase the amount matched.

4. **Know How Your Plan Works**

   By learning the basic operating rules and definitions of your 401(k) plan, you will become more comfortable about where to go to ask questions, how to monitor your investments, and how to protect your rights.

5. **Become an Informed Investor**

   Don't simply default to a safe or familiar investment option because you don't understand or don't have time to learn. It could really cost you in the long run. Get help now, whether from a professional or by doing what's necessary to educate yourself.

6. **Use the Six Concepts of Successful Investing**

   When you understand the basic investing concepts employed by financial professionals, you reduce your fear of risk and increase your probability for success.

7. **Understand Your Investment Vehicle Choices**

   Do your homework and learn about the investment choices offered in your 401(k) plan. Even if your options are few and broad-based, your selection is a very personal one. Whatever the outcome, you picked it!

8. **Build a Core Investment Portfolio**

   A core strategy keeps you on track when emotions and everyday input cloud your judgment. Once your core strategy is in place, you can fill in diversification and allocation choices with a sense of purpose.

9. **Know Where to Get Help**

   Help is out there and there's no excuse for not asking for it when you need it. It comes in different shapes and sizes, so familiarize yourself with what or who will best serve your needs.

10. **Know How to Get Your Money Out Safely**

    While it's important to know the distribution rules to minimize the impact of taxes on your 401(k) payouts, knowing the best method to take money from your plan once you've retired can determine how long your money will last.

FIGURE 1 Three stories.

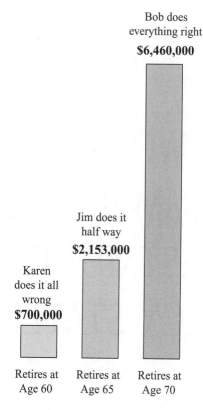

Three employees, all make $90K, all start with $100,000 in savings.
Karen, on the left, does it all wrong; 6% contribution, no match from
employer and mostly in bonds, retires early. Jim does it half way; 8%
contribution, 50% match and 50/50 stock-bond mix, and retired at 65.
Bob increases everything; maxes his contribution to 10%;
his employer chips in a 100% match. His mix is 70/25 stocks/bonds, and
he extends his retirement from age 60 to 70.

It goes without saying, your financial future is at stake. Just as your
current income is based on knowing your job, your retirement income
is dependent upon knowing, at the very least, these 10 steps. Armed
with knowledge and intention, you are relieved of worry about an emo-
tional roller coaster ride.

THE WORKING DOCUMENT: YOUR INVESTMENT POLICY STATEMENT

IN THIS APPENDIX YOU WILL LEARN HOW to clearly articulate your own personal 401(k) investment program in a workable strategy that you can implement in both good and bad markets. You might compare this to a business plan. Very few successful businesses have started and succeeded without one. Institutional investors call these "written investment plans" or "investment policy statements." You can use the same techniques. We feel that it is the critical first step.

An investment policy statement is the process that defines your financial objectives, your contribution, the company match, the amount of funds available for investment, your investment methodology and mix, and your overall strategy that will be used to reach your objectives.

This statement helps to identify your risk parameters and, thus, manages your expectations.

A written investment policy statement enables you to clearly communicate your long-term goals and objectives if you decide to work with an advisor—or it will serve as a guideline if you are implementing the investment strategy on your own. The written policy statement helps you maintain a sound long-term plan, when short-term market movements cause you to second-guess what you have learned.

We believe all 401(k) investors should have an investment policy statement that outlines their goals and how their money will be invested to reach those goals. Here's why: you are human and can get caught up in the emotion of the day. It's only through long-term planning that you are going to be successful and not fall back into old habits. In the heat of a market downturn, it is critical to have thought out your strategy ahead of time.

Creating an investment policy statement embodies the essence of the financial planning process: assessing where you are now and where you want to go and then developing a strategy to get there. Having and using this policy statement compels you to become more disciplined and systematic, increasing the probability of achieving your investment goals.

There Are Seven Steps to Establishing an Investment Policy

1. Set Your Long-Term Goals and Objectives Clearly and Concisely
Long-term goals can be anything from early retirement to purchasing a new home. One of the most common goals we have found among our clients is to be financially independent. What that often means to our clients is that their investment portfolio will provide them with the income necessary to maintain their quality of life. Identify the amount you're going to contribute, your company match, how you want to handle company stock.

2. Define the Level of Risk You Are Willing to Accept
Along the road to reaching your financial goals, there are going to be bumps caused by downturns in various markets. It is important for you to understand the amount of risk you're willing to tolerate during the investment period. In designing your portfolio, you must determine the absolute loss you're willing to accept in any one-year period without terminating your investment program. As we know, no one can predict

market movements and you have to be in a position to weather any storm.

One way to determine the level of risk in a portfolio is to look at its performance during 1973-1974, when the U.S. experienced the worst financial recession since World War II. Investors should be honest with themselves. No one can predict the future. The next two years might be similar to 1973 and 1974. There is a 5% probability that in the next 20 years we will experience a similar downturn. The Standard & Poor's 500 Index lost 37.2% and small company stocks lost 56.5%. Most investors would have a hard time maintaining a long-term perspective and staying with the program.

If you are working with a financial advisor, you can request an analysis of how your portfolio mix would have performed during 1973-74. Choose the portfolio mix with which you would have been comfortable. If you would have closed your account because of that downturn, you are taking too much risk and should consider the lower-risk model portfolio.

Investments tend to be cyclical and no one can predict their performance in the short term. The best-performing year for both the Standard & Poor's 500 Index and small company stocks was 1975, when they earned 37.2% and 65.7% respectively.

3. Establish the Expected Time Horizon
Each investor has to determine the investment period in which his or her capital will be placed. The minimum expected investment period must be at least five years for any portfolio containing equity securities. For any portfolio with less than a five-year time horizon, the portfolio should be comprised predominantly of fixed-income investments. This five-year minimum investment period is critical. The investment process must be viewed as a long-term plan for achieving the desired results. One-year volatility can be significant for many equity asset classes; however, over a five-year period, the range of returns is greatly reduced.

As Figure A-1 indicates, if you're planning to invest for a lifetime, the range of returns of a model portfolio approaches zero.

4. Determine the Rate of Return Objective
Even sophisticated investors tend to focus on their rate of return objec-

FIGURE A-1   Conservative model returns, 1972-1993.

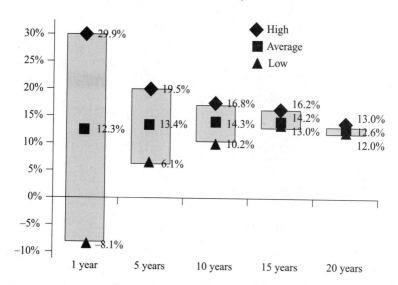

tives rather than risk. The rate of return is going to be a direct result of your willingness to take risk. In getting started, you should write down a range of returns that would be acceptable.

In Chapter 5 we identified the specific return risk profiles of each optimized model portfolio. We have reproduced these below. If you are doing this on your own, you can use these ranges of returns for each risk level as the framework to determine your return expectation for your portfolio as well as its component asset classes.

Your range should be consistent with the weighted average expected rate of return of your portfolio asset classes over the last 20 years. Don't just look at the last five years. That is likely to be an unusual period. You also want to examine some difficult market periods like 1973-1974 to see if you can stay the course (Figure A-2).

5. Select the Asset Classes to Be Utilized to Build Your Core Portfolio

In Chapters 5 and 6, we examined the asset class mutual fund types available to you. List all the asset classes that you might want to consider in your portfolio. You may be surprised with the differences between what you've been using in the past and what you should be uti-

FIGURE A-2 Asset classes, portfolios, and expected returns.

Asset Class	Expected Return
Money Market	5.82%
One-Year Fixed	7.77%
Five-Year Government	9.17%
U.S. Large Company	14.66%
U.S. Small Company	20.85%
Int'l Large Company	17.93%
Int'l Small Company	18.68%

Model	Expected Return
Defensive	10.28%
Conservative	12.63%
Moderate	14.40%
Aggressive	16.08%

lizing. Once you've identified them, you need to determine how you're going to allocate your capital to each asset class (Figure A-3).

FIGURE A-3 Allocating your portfolio.

Level of Decline	Target Growth Rate	Approximate Time Frame	Core Strategy	Riskometer
3%	3-5%	0-6 months	CDs, money markets	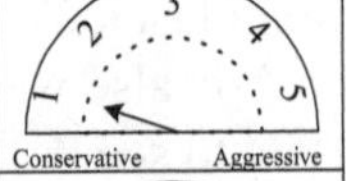
6%	5-6%	3-12 months	Bond fund, money markets, CDs, cash	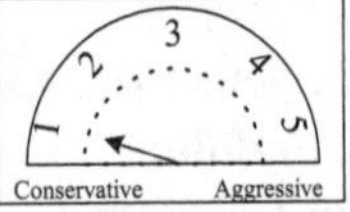
8%	6-8%	6 mos.-2 yrs.	Conservative balanced portfolio, bonds or bond funds–Portfolio 1	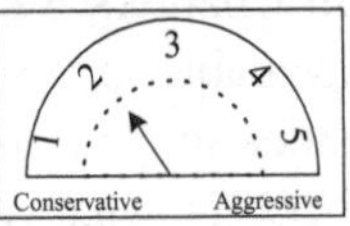

FIGURE A-3 Continued.

Level of Decline	Target Growth Rate	Approximate Time Frame	Core Strategy	Riskometer
10%	8-9%	18 mos.-3 yrs.	Balanced fund Portfolio 2	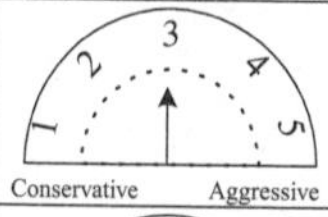
15%	9-11%	3-5 years	Conservative equity fund Portfolio 3	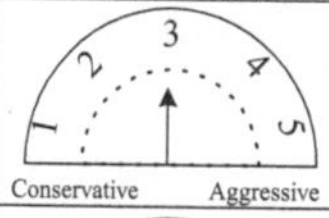
23%	10-13%	5-7 years	Equity fund Portfolio 4	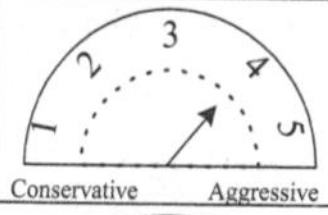
35%	11-14%	5-10 years	Equities Portfolio 4	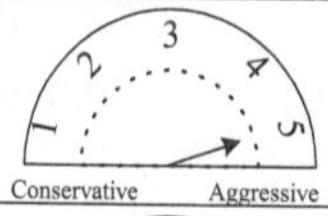
50%	12-15%	5-10 years	Equities Portfolio 4	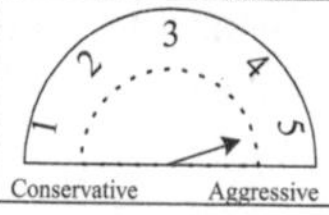

ACTION: Write down a range of returns that would be acceptable to you. You can use this range of returns for each risk level as the framework to determine your return expectation for your portfolio, as well as for the component asset classes. Now check what your company 401(k) options are and overlay this matrix.

Your Target Growth Rate _____

Make sure that your target growth rate aligns with the time horizon.

NOTES: Find your target rate of return percentage. Be aware of the level of decline you may experience and then look at your Riskometer to see what your level of risk is.

_____

_____

_____

_____

_____

6. Document the Investment Methodology to Be Utilized in Managing Your Portfolio

As we discussed in Chapter 3, there are three basic investment methodologies: security selection, market timing, and core investing. The only proven methodology for the prudent investor to use is core investing strategies.

7. Reloading or Rebalancing

This step is the one that really tests everyone's mettle. You've done an asset allocation and decided 20% here, 10% here, 5% here, 15% here—whatever it is. And then as the portfolio percolates, that allocation gets out of balance because, obviously, some parts of the portfolio do better than others.

Hopefully you've built your portfolio to have negative correlation and that balances out your risks. So now, all of a sudden, instead of 20%-20%-20% in each group, one group is at 30% and the other is at 10% and the other is at 20%-20%. Prudence would tell you to take the 30% and make it 20% and take the 10% and make it 20%. I think that's the biggest problem people have, because you're asking them to take from the portfolio that's doing well and put it into the one that's not. This is the most basic form of contrariness there is. But that's what rebalancing is—and it's sometimes a tough decision.

One issue I've never really resolved is at what point do you rebalance or reload? If your portfolio is off 5% from your initial allocation, do you rebalance at that point? Or do you wait until it's off 10% or 15% and do it at the end of the year? My rule of thumb is probably a little different from other people's. It's more of a gut feeling.

To be a successful investor, you must take full responsibility for your investment portfolio decisions. Being responsible, however, does not mean that you need to become a bona fide expert in portfolio theory and make all the difficult asset allocation decisions yourself. Instead, you need to familiarize yourself sufficiently with the operating rules contained within this book and determine whether you should manage your portfolio on your own or seek a competent investment advisor to assist you in the implementation of your plan. The written policy statement will enable you to better define your investment expectations and put you in a position to decide how best to implement your asset class portfolio. If you hire an investment advisor, you will be better able to supervise your financial advisor.

B

THE HISTORY OF
401(k) PLANS

THE 401(K) RETIREMENT PLAN EVOLVED OUT of the pension fund industry. In the '70s, most companies were running their own pension funds through the local banks. It was a very unprofessional, casual sort of management, but it was the only game in town. Prior to 1974, a company could have a pension fund that wasn't really backed by anything. If the company went out of business, the pension evaporated. In those days, there were no 401(k)s and IRAs hadn't been invented. For retirement, most people relied on Social Security, a pension plan, or a combination of both, and very few people truly understood how their plans worked. Most employees just assumed their company was going to pay them a certain amount of money per year. They had no idea where the money was coming from. Because of that, there were lots of abuses.

Corporations lost money; retirees lost money. The system was out of control, so the federal government stepped in. In 1974, the government mandated that it was unfair for somebody to work at a company for 20 or 30 years and then lose their retirement benefits. The government informed employers that they had to fund employees' retirement plans, putting money aside so that, if the company went bankrupt, employees were still guaranteed pensions.

Enter the ERISA

As a result, Congress passed the Employee Retirement Income Security Act (ERISA), and it changed the rules of investing forever. ERISA created huge, rapidly growing pools of money, which, in turn, attracted bright people to manage the money. Investment managers started breaking away from the banks and became professional asset managers. These money managers gave the people what they wanted: a very diversified, very conscious method of winning and losing in the market over short and long-term time periods while paying no taxes and competing for every last basis point of total return.

The Act outlined rules and determined how much money must be allocated for pension funds based on how many employees a corporation had. It further stipulated that anything done with this pool of money must be for the benefit of the employees. As that was the only consideration, it eliminated the inherent conflict of interest that results when a company tries to serve itself and its retirees at the same time.

> The prudent investor rule states that any investment selection may be made, provided that a review of the decision at a later date would determine that, with the information available at the time, the choice was a prudent one.

Unfortunately, this Act did not tell corporations how to manage their money, but it did state that the trustees of a pension fund were fiduciaries and therefore were personally responsible for their actions. It mandated that they be guided by the *prudent investor rule*.

The prudent investor rule states that any investment selection may be made, provided that a review of the decision at a later date would determine that, with the information available at the time, the choice was a prudent one. It didn't give specifics, but it gave enough guidance so that corporations knew they'd better have an audit trail; their decisions had better make sense, even to someone looking at them 10 or 20 years in the future. If any employee later claimed that they didn't get the pension they were entitled to, the corporation would be able to prove that, given the circumstances at the time, their actions were prudent.

Problems with Pension Funds

Generally, management of the pension fund was handed to the top executives, where it was treated as a part-time job. Not surprisingly, business owners and corporate heads didn't want to be saddled with these fiduciary responsibilities of pension fund management. "We're *not* in the business of managing money," they complained. "Let's get somebody who knows what this prudent investor rule thing is so we don't get sued or lose our good jobs." Their main goal was to avoid any liability to their employees or embarrassment in front of their Board of Directors if the Dow Jones was up 10%, but the fund was down 5%.

Since the administrator's job was directly linked to the pension fund's performance, many administrators decided to stick with safe, predictable, fixed-income investments that generally under-performed to the stock market averages, so pension funds became very conservative. Most included a mixture of CDs, bonds, and fixed-income vehicles. Bonds were considered safe, and safety was the name of the game, so the plan administrator would usually put 70% or more of the money in fixed income.

If the administrator reported annualized returns of at least 6% or 7% every quarter, they weren't embarrassed and got to keep their job and didn't get personally sued. They had to assure that the promised retirement payments were not at risk and that the investments were safe. They didn't have to be concerned with volatility of principal or with the effects of inflation since their retirement obligations were a fixed amount. Back then, bonds were priced at par ($1000) and most administrators simply reported their value at par so they sailed along looking good, earning reasonable rates of interest.

Professional Money Managers

Pension plan administrators weren't focused on making money; they were focused on *not* getting sued and not losing money. However, ERISA provided that, if they hired someone to manage the money, all they had to do was monitor their actions—sort of, "peek in and see how things were doing." But, companies were also obligated to grow their retirement plan assets. Since there was such little growth in the fixed-income investments, they hired professional money managers to handle the equity portion of their fund. So far, so good—except safety was still the name of the game. For many corporations, it was too risky to let one manager handle the entire equity portion of their pension fund so, to be safe, they hired five or six money managers.

> Pension plan administrators weren't focused on making money; they were focused on *not* getting sued and not losing money.

Back then few CFOs knew enough about diversification to hire money managers fluent in different investment styles or categories. So they just brought in five managers, instead of one, and assumed that each would take a different approach. More than once, one manager was selling the same stock that the other managers were buying; but, no one understood investment theory too well back then.

Differentiating Investment Styles

Then in the 1980s, investment *styles* entered the equation as funds were identified as growth, value, international, small cap, large cap and so on. Corporations started investing in the international marketplaces, and were met with resistance at first because the boards of directors wanted to invest in only American stocks. But companies like Toyota or Sony were undeniably good investments, so the resistance began to disappear.

It was a logical step, but still it took years to get American companies to go global with their pension investments, because international investments were perceived as riskier than American investments. The real clincher came when it was pointed out that foreign markets didn't correlate with the U.S. stock market, thereby ensuring broader diversification. As pension plan administrators became more knowledgeable about volatility and more comfortable with investing in foreign equities, the percentage of equities inside pension plans increased to upwards of 50% or 60%.

The Era of Personal Responsibility—401(k)

But then something happened. A pension consultant by the name of Ted Benna changed the game. He found a loophole in the Revenue Act of 1978—in Section 401, Paragraph (k)—and designed an entirely new type of pension plan. A change in the law allowed money to be withdrawn from employee paychecks before taxes, invested, and allowed to grow tax-free. He knew tax savings alone would not be sufficient incentive for many employees to participate in the plan, so he designed the plan so that the companies could match contributions and the plan would be portable—when employees changed jobs, they could take it with them. It was the beginning of the Era of Personal Responsibility.

This idea hit about the same time another era, when employees worked at one company for 40 years and then retired with a gold watch and a full pension, was ending. People were changing jobs more often, and corporation presidents were eager to rid themselves of pension plan liability. Companies began to move away from defined benefit plans and toward this new form of defined contribution plans called, simply, the 401(k) plan. Guess who loved these changes? All the corporate executives who had been told they might be personally sued if the old pension plans didn't perform.

This 401(k) plan idea put the investment decisions on the shoulders of the participant. The company could put pre-tax contributions into special investment accounts where the money could grow tax-deferred until withdrawn during retirement. Employers could also contribute to their employees' accounts, which was a great way for them to offer an additional benefit while drastically reducing both the cost and liability associated with traditional pension plans.

This was a great new idea, so just about every big corporation started a 401(k) because there was no liability. The other plus was they didn't have to worry about calculating retirement benefits. The new rules under the 401(k) were "Whatever you have, you have." This was an admirable idea, but it made the least informed person (the participant) the investment decision maker.

And, as a result, these newly empowered employees, like the first wave of pension plan administrators, put all their money into fixed-income investments because they were thought to be safe. In the early days of 401(k) plans, 80% of employee contributions were invested in money market funds and bond funds.

That started to change when mutual funds launched intense advertising campaigns aimed at the 401(k) market. Suddenly, retirement plans were offering 8% loaded funds to investors, a strategy that was easy for plan sponsors because the mutual fund was the easiest way to handle all the record-keeping responsibilities.

Fidelity

And then Fidelity arrived! Seemingly overnight, Fidelity revolutionized the 401(k) marketplace. In the late 1980s, Fidelity simply went to the market place and said, "We have mutual funds which participants can track daily, a 1-800 phone number, daily valuation, great communications, and good investment results." This was perfect timing, because in the late 1980s, the top reason for a company to switch record keepers was investment alternatives built in the plan, along with full record-keeping services. They called these "bundled" plans.

> And then Fidelity arrived! Seemingly overnight, Fidelity revolutionized the 401(k) marketplace.

Fidelity was the first company to grasp the new rules and build a business around them—turnkey, full service, full administration, full investment options, and administrative capabilities. Because of the economies of size, Fidelity Investments eliminated sales loads. Educational campaigns were started to get participants to invest in equity funds that had higher fees and made more money for the fund company.

The Bull Market and Risk

Around this same time, the greatest bull market in history began, with investors coming to the conclusion that equity mutual fund returns would keep going up and up forever. From 1989 to 1999, the market never stopped growing. 401(k) participants couldn't get enough mutual funds; and, since all equity mutual funds were generally rising in value, frankly, the participants really didn't have to know that much. New mutual funds sprang up overnight and quickly became the most popular investment in 401(k) plans. Today, there are more registered mutual funds than registered stocks on the New York Stock Exchange.

While this bull market was taking place, investors were clamoring for the next great investment idea. Financial advice magazines flourished and TV networks were created that provided investing "news" 24 hours a day. It didn't matter that most journalists had no personal experience in the stock markets or financial education; whatever they said became "fact" at the office water cooler—even if it was contradictory at best, or totally misleading at worst. The common perception was that it was easy to achieve double digit returns by just selecting the "hot" investment of the day.

In that market, how could you lose? Risk had heretofore been described as bad and something investors should attempt to avoid. Now all that mattered was that the more risk an investor took, the greater returns they were guaranteed to receive. No one talked about "modern portfolio theory" or the "efficient market hypothesis"; or that it was academically proven that it was difficult, if not impossible, to outperform the market. Missing was the recognition that this great bull market would end sometime, and that, to the degree of risk undertaken, dire consequences might be the result.

Today, as we have seen the Nasdaq bubble burst and 401(k) participants have seen the value of their portfolios erode, risk has been discovered to be something that must be understood and should be controlled through various strategies. Not all has been lost, and there are still great opportunities for investors, now smarter from experience, to recover past market losses. For example, time is on our side, with demographic trends of increasing longevity indicating life expectancy at now over age 76. Individuals are staying in the workplace longer, and a longer earning cycle means a longer savings cycle.

What About Our "Social Security"?

With one of the largest-ever demographics ("baby boomers") of our society arriving at retirement age, our overall longer life expectancies, and a higher expected standard of living in retirement, Social Security has become the topic of serious concern. What most people don't realize is that Social Security was never set up to be a retirement plan, but as a safety net.

When Social Security was instituted in 1935 during the Depression years, there were 33 workers for every one retiree. Working people would pay a small portion of their wages into the Social Security system with the idea that the current working population would support the retirees of that time. So money went in and right back out again. A person retiring at age 65 had a seven-year life expectancy. Today, a person is expected to live a full 16 years after retirement.

By the 1960s, the ratio had already dropped to 15 workers for every one person retired. It's estimated that in the year 2030, there will be only two and a half workers for every one person retired. Some have estimated it would require a contribution of at least 20% of every worker's income for the system just to be kept alive.

Though Social Security may survive, you won't be able to rely solely upon it to provide a decent retirement income. This 401(k) plan you look at every once in a while may end up as your only source of retirement income. You may have to save at a higher rate, achieve a higher rate of return on your savings, or do both in order to maintain a reasonable standard of living in old age.

It's All Up to You

So, one thing should now be clear. The responsibility to achieve adequate retirement assets rests on the individual. Individuals must make every effort to understand fundamental investment concepts such as risk and return, asset allocation, effective diversification, the power of compounding, and monitoring and adjusting their accounts; as well as manage the available opportunities to their best advantage, including their 401(k) plans.

We have everything going for us now: very low inflation, low interest rates, tax incentives, expansionary monetary and fiscal policy, and low energy policy. All the ingredients are there for a long business cycle again, which means the environment to accumulate wealth could be very good. So, get started!

C

GLOSSARY OF TERMS

401(k) plan A defined contribution plan that permits employees to have a portion of their salary deducted from their paycheck and contributed to an account. Federal (and sometimes state) taxes on the employee contributions and investment earnings are deferred until the participant receives a distribution from the plan (typically at retirement). Employers may also make contributions to a participant's account.

actual contribution percentage (ACP) A non-discrimination test that compares the amount deferred by highly compensated employees with the deferrals of non-highly compensated employees, required if the plan provides for employer matching contributions.

actual deferral percentage (ADP) A non-discrimination test that compares the amount deferred by highly compensated employees with the deferrals of non-highly compensated employees.

allocation The employer's contribution to a defined contribution plan.

alternate payee A person other than a plan participant (such as a spouse, former spouse, child, etc.) who, under a qualified domestic relations order, has a right to receive all or some of a participant's pension benefits.

annual audit Federal law requires that all plans with more than 100 participants be audited by an independent auditor. It is also common to refer to a Department of Labor or IRS examination of a plan as a plan audit.

annual report A document filed annually (Form 5500) with the IRS that reports pension plan information for a particular year, including such items as participation, funding, and administration.

annuity A contract providing retirement income at regular intervals. See also *qualified joint and survivor annuity*.

automatic deferral default percentage The percentage of pay that is deferred when an employee is enrolled in a plan through its automatic enrollment feature. The typical automatic deferral default percentage is 3% of pay. Participants can generally choose to defer an amount other than the default percentage.

automatic enrollment The practice of enrolling all eligible employees in a plan and beginning participant deferrals without requiring the employees to submit a request to participate. Plan design specifies how these automatic deferrals will be invested. Employees who do not want to make deferrals to the plan must actively file a request to be excluded from the plan. Participants can generally change the amount of pay that is deferred and how it is invested.

Barra—S&P 500/Barra Value Index An index designed to differentiate between fast-growing companies and slower-growing or undervalued companies. Standard & Poor's and Barra cooperate to employ a price to book value calculation, whereby the market capitalization of an index (S&P 500, S&P MidCap 400, S&P SmallCap 600) is divided equally between growth and value. The growth and value definitions are only available on the U.S. indices. The indices are rebalanced twice per year.

beneficiary A person, persons, or trust designated to receive the plan benefits of a participant in the event of the participant's death.

book value The common stock equity of a company as it appears on a balance sheet: total assets minus liabilities, preferred stock, and intangible assets such as goodwill.

cafeteria plan In this plan employees may choose from a "menu" of two or more benefits.

cash or deferred arrangement (CODA) A type of profit-sharing or stock bonus plan in which employees may defer current pre-tax compensation.

cash or deferred election A participant request to defer compensation, on a pre-tax basis, to a CODA plan.

cash-out The distribution of assets from a qualified plan to a participant prior to retirement, typically occurring when a participant has a balance under $5,000 and leaves a company without requesting to have his or her assets rolled over into an IRA or into a new employer's plan. Cash-outs are subject to federal withholding tax and are subject to the 10% early withdrawal penalty if not rolled over.

cash profit-sharing plan A type of profit-sharing plan in which the company makes contributions directly to employees in cash or stock. (This type of profit-sharing plan is not a qualified retirement plan.)

core strategy A core strategy is the base or beginning structure of an investment portfolio that includes two or more asset classes other than cash. This term can apply to any kind of portfolio that uses fixed-income (bonds) as well as equity securities to reach stated investor goals. Most mutual funds use a core strategy in selecting their initial stocks within their portfolios as outlined in the investment objectives. Core is the base on which all investment management strategies are built.

conversion The process of changing from one service provider to another.

deferred profit-sharing plan A type of qualified retirement plan in which the company makes contributions to individual participant accounts.

defined benefit plan A retirement plan in which the sponsoring company provides a certain guaranteed benefit to participants based on a pre-determined formula.

defined contribution plan An employer-sponsored plan in which contributions are made to individual participant accounts and the final benefit consists solely of assets (including investment returns) that have accumulated in these individual accounts. Depending on the type of defined contribution plan, contributions may be made by the company, the participant, or both.

Department of Labor (DOL) The U.S. Department of Labor (DOL) deals with issues related to the American workforce—including topics concerning pension and benefit plans. Through its branch agency, the Pension and Welfare Benefits Administration, the DOL is responsible for administering the provisions of Title I of the Employee Retirement Income Security Act (ERISA).

determination letter Document issued by the IRS formally recognizing that the plan meets the qualifications for tax-advantaged treatment.

disclosure Plan sponsors must provide plan participants with access to certain types of information, including the summary plan descriptions, summary of material modifications, and summary annual reports.

discrimination testing Tax-qualified retirement plans must be administered in compliance with several regulations requiring numerical measurements. Typically, the process of determining whether the plan is in compliance is collectively called discrimination testing.

distribution Any payout made from a retirement plan. See also *lump-sum distribution* and *annuity*.

early withdrawal penalty There is a 10% penalty tax for withdrawal of assets from a qualified retirement plan prior to retirement. This 10% penalty tax is in addition to regular federal and (if applicable) state tax.

eligibility Conditions that must be met in order to participate in a plan, such as age or service requirements.

eligible employees Employees who meet the requirements for participation in an employer-sponsored plan.

employee stock ownership plan (ESOP) A qualified defined contribution plan in which plan assets are invested primarily or exclusively in the securities of the sponsoring employer.

ERISA The Employee Retirement Income Security Act, a federal law passed in 1974 to regulate the design and administration of private pension plans. Among its statutes, ERISA calls for proper plan reporting and disclosure to participants.

ERISA Rights Statement   The Employee Retirement Income Security Act (ERISA) requires that this document, explaining participant and beneficiary rights, be included within a summary plan description (SPD).

ESOP   See *employee stock ownership plan*.

excess aggregate contributions   After-tax participant contributions or matching employer contributions that cause a plan to fail the 401(m) actual contribution percentage (ACP) non-discrimination test.

excess benefit plan   A plan, or part of a plan, maintained to provide benefits that exceed IRS Code 415 limits on contributions and benefits.

excess contributions   Pre-tax participant contributions that cause a plan to fail the 401(k) actual deferral percentage (ADP) non-discrimination test or the actual contribution percentage (ACP)

excludable employees   The employees who may be excluded from the group being tested during 401(k) nondiscrimination testing. The following are excludable employees: certain ex-employees, certain airline pilots, non-resident aliens with no U.S. source of income, employees who do not meet minimum age and service plan requirements, and employees whose retirement benefits are covered by collective bargaining agreements.

expense ratio   The percentage of a fund's assets that are used to pay its annual expenses.

facts and circumstances test   The test determining whether financial need exists for a 401(k) hardship withdrawal.

fidelity bond   Protects participants in the event a fiduciary or other responsible person steals or mishandles plan assets.

fiduciary   A person with the authority to make decisions regarding a plan's assets or important administrative matters. Fiduciaries are required under the Employee Retirement Income Security Act (ERISA) to make decisions based solely on the best interests of plan participants.

fiduciary insurance   Insurance that protects plan fiduciaries in the event that they are found liable for a breach of fiduciary responsibility.

forfeiture   Plan assets surrendered by participants upon termination of employment before being fully vested in the plan. Forfeitures may be distributed to the other participants in the plan or used to offset employer contributions.

Form 1099R A form sent to the recipient of a plan distribution and filed with the IRS listing the amount of the distribution.

Form 5500 A form that all qualified retirement plans (excluding SEPs and SIMPLE IRAs) must file annually with the IRS.

guaranteed investment contract (GIC) A contract between an insurance company and a qualified retirement plan, like a 401(k). The contract guarantees a specific rate of return (i.e., stable value) over a specified period of time. GICs or stable value funds are a conservative way of guaranteeing a certain rate of return on your money. What is guaranteed is the rate of return on the contract, not the principal investment. This reality hit investors hard in the early 1990s, when three insurers failed to meet their GIC commitments because of bankruptcy.

hardship or in-service distribution At the employer's option, a participant's withdrawal of his or her plan contributions prior to retirement. Eligibility may be conditioned on the presence of financial hardship. These distributions are taxable as early distributions and are subject to a 10% penalty tax if the participant is under age 59½.

highly compensated employee (HCE) An HCE, according to the Small Business Job Protection Act of 1996, is an employee who received more than $80,000 in compensation (indexed annually, raised to $90,000 for 2002) during the last plan year *or* is a 5% owner in the company.

individual retirement account/arrangement (IRA) Personal retirement vehicle in which a person can make annual tax-deductible contributions. These accounts must meet IRS Code 408 requirements, but are created and funded at the discretion of the employee. They are not sponsored by the employer.

Internal Revenue Service (IRS) This branch of the U.S. Treasury Department is responsible for administering the requirements of qualified pension plans and other retirement vehicles. The IRS also worked with the Department of Labor and the Pension and Welfare Benefits Administration to develop Form 5500 and is now responsible for monitoring the data submitted annually on Form 5500 reports.

Keogh plan A qualified defined contribution plan permitting self-employed individuals to contribute a portion of their earnings pre-tax to an individual account.

KSOP A plan arrangement that includes both 401(k) contributions and an *employee stock ownership plan* (ESOP).

lifestyle fund A mutual fund that invests in a range of asset classes, based on the age of the investor, forming a complete investment portfolio.

lump-sum distribution The distribution at retirement of a participant's entire account balance.

matching contribution A contribution made by the company to the account of the participant in ratio to contributions made by the participant.

material modification A change in the terms of the plan that may affect plan participants, or other changes in a summary plan description (SPD).

median market cap An indicator of the size of companies in which a mutual fund invests.

money market fund A mutual fund seeking to generate income for participants through investments in short-term securities.

money-purchase plan A type of defined contribution plan in which the employer's contributions are determined by a specific formula, usually as a percentage of pay. Contributions are not dependent on company profits.

multi-employer plan A pension plan to which more than one employer contributes and that is maintained according to collective bargaining agreements.

mutual fund An account with a broad range of investment options, each of which is diversified, reducing the risk to the participant.

named fiduciary Any person specified in the plan document as having the authority to control and manage the operation of the plan. The plan document must name one or more fiduciaries, who must be identified as fiduciaries by a procedure specified in the plan document.

net asset value (NAV) The dollar value of a single mutual fund share, calculated at the end of each business day. It's based on the value of the fund's underlying assets minus its liabilities, divided by the number of shares outstanding.

non-elective contribution An employer contribution that cannot be withdrawn or paid to the employee in cash. This contribution is neither a matching contribution nor an elective contribution.

non-highly compensated employees (NHCEs) A group of employees determined on the basis of compensation or ownership interest. See *highly compensated employees*.

non-qualified deferred compensation plan A plan subject to tax, in which the assets of certain employees (usually highly compensated employees) are deferred. These funds may be reached by an employer's creditors.

participant-directed account A plan that allows participants to select their own investment options.

party-in-interest A person or an organization with a relationship to the plan. Parties-in-interest to a plan include the employer; the directors, officers, employees, or owners of the employer; any employee organization whose members are plan participants; plan fiduciaries; and plan service providers. Parties-in-interest are prohibited from entering into certain transactions with the plan.

P/E ratio See *price/earnings ratio*.

Pension and Welfare Benefits Administration (PWBA) A branch of the Department of Labor that protects the pensions, health plans, and other employee benefits of American workers. The PWBA enforces Title I of the Employee Retirement Income Security Act (ERISA), which contains rules for reporting and disclosure, vesting, participation, funding, and fiduciary conduct.

Pension Benefit Guaranty Corporation (PBGC) A federal agency established by Title IV of the Employee Retirement Income Security Act (ERISA) for the insurance of defined benefit pension plans. The PBGC provides payment of pension benefits if a plan terminates and is unable to cover all required benefits.

plan administrator The individual, group, or corporation named in the plan document as responsible for day-to-day operations. The plan sponsor is generally the plan administrator if no other entity is named.

plan document   A report that outlines in detail how a 401(k) plan operates, with legal information about the plan. The law requires every 401(k) to have a plan document. In fact, the *plan* in *plan document* is why 401(k)s are called 401(k) *plans*. The law also requires that a summary of the plan document be provided to employees (the summary plan description).

plan loan   Loan from a participant's accumulated plan assets, not to exceed 50% of the balance or $50,000, whichever is less. This is an optional plan feature.

plan participant   Person who has an account in the plan and any beneficiaries who may be eligible to receive an account balance.

plan sponsor   The entity responsible for establishing and maintaining the plan.

plan year   The calendar, policy, or fiscal year for which plan records are maintained.

portability   The ability to transfer funds from one type of defined contribution plan to another when, upon termination of employment, an employee transfers pension funds from one employer's plan to another or to an IRA without penalty.

price/book (price to book) ratio   The share price of a stock divided by its net worth, or book value, per share.

price/earnings (P/E) ratio   The ratio of a stock's current price to its earnings per share over the past year.   The P/E ratio of a fund is the weighted average of the P/E ratios of the stocks it holds.

profit-sharing plan   Company-sponsored plan funded only by company contributions. Company contributions may be determined by a fixed formula related to the employer's profits or may be at the discretion of the board of directors.

prohibited transaction   Any of the activities regarding treatment of plan assets by fiduciaries that are prohibited by the Employee Retirement Income Security Act (ERISA). These include transactions with a party-in-interest, including the sale, exchange, lease, or loan of plan securities or other properties. Any treatment of plan assets by a fiduciary that is not consistent with the best interests of the plan participants is a prohibited transaction.

PWBA See *Pension and Welfare Benefits Administration.*

qualified domestic relations order (QDRO) A judgment, decree, or order that creates or recognizes the right of someone other than the plan participant (such as former spouse, child, etc.) to receive all or a portion of a participant's retirement plan benefits.

qualified joint and survivor annuity (QJSA) An annuity with payments continuing to the surviving spouse after the participant's death, equal to at least 50% of the participant's benefit.

qualified plan Any plan that qualifies for favorable tax treatment by meeting the requirements of section 401(a) of the Internal Revenue Code and by following applicable regulations. It includes 401(k) and deferred profit-sharing plans.

rollover The action of moving plan assets from one qualified plan to another or to an IRA within 60 days of distributions, while retaining the tax benefits of a qualified plan.

r-squared A measure of how closely a fund's performance correlates with the performance of the market overall or a benchmark index. It ranges from 0 to 1 (or 100), with 0 indicating no correlation and 1 (or 100) indicating perfect correlation.

safe harbor rules Provisions that exempt certain individuals or kinds of companies from one or more regulations.

salary reduction plan A retirement plan that permits an employee to set aside a portion of earned income in a tax-deferred account selected by the employer. Contributions made to the account and income earned from investing contributions are sheltered from taxes until the funds are withdrawn. Also called *401(k) plan.*

Savings Incentive Match Plan for Employees (SIMPLE) A type of defined contribution plan for employers with 100 or fewer employees in which the employer matches 100% of employee salary deferrals up to 3% of compensation or provides non-elective contributions up to 2% of compensation. These contributions, which are immediately and 100% vested, are the only employer contribution to the plan. SIMPLE plans may be structured as IRAs or as 401(k) plans.

Schedule SSA A form that must be filed by all plans subject to the Employee Retirement Income Security Act (ERISA) Section 203 minimum vesting requirements. The schedule, which is attached to

Form 5500, provides data on participants who separated from service with a vested benefit but were not paid their benefits.

SEP   See *Simplified Employee Pension plan.*

service provider   A company that provides any type of service to the plan, including managing assets, record keeping, providing plan education, and administering the plan.

SIMPLE Plan   See *Savings Incentive Match Plan for Employees.*

Simplified Employee Pension plan (SEP)   A defined contribution plan in which employers make contributions to individual employee accounts (similar to IRAs). Employees may also make pre-tax contributions to these accounts. As of January 1997, no new SEP plans may be formed.

SPD   See *summary plan description.*

stock bonus plan   A defined contribution plan in which company contributions are distributable in the form of company stock.

summary of material modifications   A document that must be distributed to plan participants summarizing material modifications made to a plan. See *material modification.*

summary plan description (SPD)   A document describing the features of an employer-sponsored plan. The primary purpose of the SPD is to disclose the features of the plan to current and potential plan participants. The Employee Retirement Income Security Act (ERISA) requires that the SPD contain certain information, including participant rights under ERISA, claims procedures, and funding arrangements.

target benefit plan   A type of defined contribution plan in which company contributions are based on an actuarial valuation designed to provide a target benefit to each participant upon retirement. The plan does not guarantee that such benefit will be paid; its only obligation is to pay whatever benefit can be provided by the amount in the participant's account. It is a hybrid of a money-purchase plan and a defined benefit plan.

tax-sheltered annuity (TSA)   A supplemental retirement savings program authorized by section 403(b) of the Internal Revenue Code. Also known as a 403(b) plan, a TSA provides a tax shelter for

501(c)(3) tax-exempt employers (including educational or charitable organizations). Employers qualifying for a TSA may defer taxes on contributions to certain annuity contracts or custodial accounts.

top-heavy plan A plan in which 60% of account balances (both vested and non-vested) are held by highly compensated employees.

trustee The individual, bank, or trust company having fiduciary responsibility for holding plan assets.

turnover rate For a mutual fund, a measure of the trading activity.

vesting The plan participants' right to company contributions that have accrued in their individual accounts.

vesting schedule The structure for determining participants' rights to company contributions that have accrued in their individual accounts. In a plan with immediate vesting, company contributions are fully vested as soon as they are deposited to a participant's account. Cliff vesting provides that company contributions will be fully vested only after a specific amount of time; employees who leave before this point will not be entitled to any of the company contributions (with certain exceptions for retirees). In plans with graduated vesting, vesting occurs in specified increments.

I N D E X

401(k) plans
  calculator, 112
  checking for mistakes, 43-44
  components, 38
  creation, 155-156
  defined, 1, 36
  distributions, rules, 125-132
  and Economic Growth and Tax
    Relief Reconciliation Act of
    2001, 9
  eligibility, 17-18
  enrollment, automatic, 17
  evaluating, 44-46
  fiduciaries, 37, 38, 42, 43, 152-153
  for goals other than retirement, 23-24
  history, 151-159
  liquidation, 41-42
  loans, 133-137
  participation statistics, 9-10
  process, 38-43
  protection, legal, 42-43
  rollover, 126-130
  self-directed, 41, 43
  trouble, warning signs, 45-46
  withdrawals, 137-139
  See also SIMPLE
403(b) account
  and rollovers, 126-130
  and Section 72(t) distributions,
    131-132
457 pension plan, and rollovers, 126-130

A

administrator, plan
  defined, 37

early years, 153-154
advisors
  financial, choosing, 122-124
  financial, community, 116-124
  financial, consulting, 113-116
  financial, independent fee-only,
    described, 120
  financial, payment, 121-122
  institutional investment, as invest-
    ment managers, 40
allocation, asset
  and asset classes, 65-68
  bonds vs. stocks, 103
  and Brinson, Hood, and Beebower
    study, 63-64
  and core portfolio, 103-111, 147-149
  defined, 63
  vs. diversification, 63
  explained, 63-65
  of portfolio, 51-57
  rebalancing, 68-73, 149
  stocks vs. bonds, 103
  stocks, growth vs. value, 103-106
  strategic, 64
  tactical, 64-65
American College, 117
American Consumer Credit
  Counseling, and credit card debt,
  14-15
American Institute of Certified Public
  Accountants
  designation, 118
  information, 121
annuities, and 401(k) distribution, 130
asset allocation, *see* allocation, asset

Larry Chambers is a writer specializing in the business and finance area. He has written or ghostwritten over 30 books and 800 articles and has built an infrastructure of over 50,000 pages of research and material that gives him industry depth and investment knowledge. Previously Larry was a stockbroker at E.F. Hutton & Co. and Dean Witter. While at Hutton, he achieved an outstanding track record, was named one of the top 10 brokers out of more than 5,000, and received numerous awards for his work. He was also an Army Ranger sergeant with L Co. 75th Ranger, 101st Airborne Division and is a graduate of the University of Utah.

Ken Zeisenheim is managing director of Thornburg Investment Management Company, the manager and advisor for Thornburg mutual funds, and serves as president of Thornburg Securities Corporation, the distributor of Thornburg Funds. Prior to joining Thornburg in mid-1995, Ken was the senior vice president of mutual fund marketing at Raymond James & Associates. Ken also held a variety of other positions at Raymond James, including senior vice president of financial planning and financial services. He also served as president of Planning Corporation of America (wholly owned insurance marketing subsidiary) and first vice president of sales for all Raymond James offices outside the state of Florida.